To Sheneen —
~~Lift~~-~~up~~!
With gratitude and in friendship,
Susan

To Sheneen —

To a great friend
and colleague
Best wishes.

Tom Heymann

Lifting People Up

THE POWER OF RECOGNITION

Additional Books by the Authors

CO-AUTHORED BOOKS
Apples Are Square: Thinking Differently About Leadership

Values-Based Leadership

ALSO BY SUSAN SMITH KUCZMARSKI
Becoming A Happy Family: Pathways to the Family Soul

The Sacred Flight of the Teenager: A Parent's Guide to Stepping Back and Letting Go

The Family Bond: Inspiring Tips for Creating a Closer Family

ALSO BY THOMAS D. KUCZMARSKI
Innovating Chicago Style

Innovation

Managing New Products

Innovating the Corporation

Lifting People Up

THE POWER OF RECOGNITION

Susan Smith Kuczmarski, Ed.D.
Thomas D. Kuczmarski

BOOK ENDS
PUBLISHING

Cataloging information available from the Library of Congress

Book Ends Publishing
Chicago, IL 60614

Publisher: Book Ends Publishing

Editor, Jacob T. Sherman

Cover design by Rui Weidt/Tanen Directed Advertising

Page design by Linda Kornmeyer/Tanen Directed Advertising

Printed in the United States of America

This book is dedicated to our three adult sons,
John, James and Thomas Kuczmarski.

TABLE OF CONTENTS

SECTION 1: LIFT UP

SECTION 2: UNLEASH THE LEADER WITHIN

SECTION 3: CREATE A HIGH-PERFORMING CULTURE

INDEX

ABOUT THE AUTHORS

Lifting People Up: The Power of Recognition is the authors' third collaborative book on the topic of leadership. In 1995, they wrote their pioneering *Values-Based Leadership*, which launched the values in the workplace movement. In 2007, they co-authored *Apples Are Square: Thinking Differently About Leadership*, which reveals the power of six leadership qualities—humility, compassion, transparency, inclusiveness and values-based decisiveness.

Susan Smith Kuczmarski, Ed.D. is a globally

recognized authority and speaker on values-based leadership. Her teach-

 ing and research currently focus on: How Values and Norms Impact Culture and Leadership, Building Innovation Leadership, and New Leadership for an Innovative Edge. For the past ten years, she has been a Lecturer in the executive education program at the Kellogg School of Management at Northwestern University. She currently teaches in Kellogg's "Creating and Leading A Culture of Innovation" program. During the course of a career that spans more than three decades, she has taught at nine universities, worked in three nonprofits, including the United Nations, and co-founded the Chicago-based consulting firm, Kuczmarski Innovation, which provides thought–leadership on innovation, culture and values. She currently serves as the Chairman of the Board of Trustees of the Chicago City Day School and a mentor for 1871, Chicago's entrepreneurial hub for digital startups.

Trained as a cultural anthropologist, Dr. Kuczmarski has done extensive research on the question of how leadership skills are learned and put into practice. She specializes in developing innovative leadership programs, conducting ethnographic research, building team energy, guiding shared leadership, and understanding organizational culture. Known for her interactive teaching style, she offers creative leadership seminars for corporate, non-profit and educational groups. Her approach to leadership training champions an innovative skill set. It includes knowing self, finding common ground, letting creativity reign, and rooting for and serving others.

She is the author of six award-winning books, three on leadership (co-authored with Tom Kuczmarski) and three on families. *Values-Based Leadership*, Prentice Hall, 1995), pioneered the expression of personal values in the workplace. *Apples Are Square: Thinking Differently About Leadership* (Kaplan Publishing, 2007) received the coveted "2007 Best Business Book" from *Fast Company Magazine*. In 2012, global leader, Deepak Chopra, wrote the Foreword to the Second Edition of *Apples Are Square*. Enthusiastically received, the book has been printed in various languages, including editions in China, Taiwan and South Korea.

Becoming A Happy Family: Pathways to the Family Soul (Book Ends Publishing, 2015) was awarded the IPPY Gold Medal and Eric Hoffer Book Awards. It serves as a guide to find the "sticky glue" that supports the family bond and deepen connections across the family network. It lays out six family strengtheners—humor, emotion, acceptance, renewal, togetherness and struggle. Her best-selling, *The Sacred Flight of the Teenager: A Parent's Guide to Stepping Back and Letting Go* (Book Ends Publishing, 2003), received the prestigious "Seal of Approval" Award from the National Parenting Center and a *Book of the Year Award* from ForeWord Magazine. To encourage family relationship building, she wrote *The Family Bond: Inspiring Tips for Creating a Closer Family* (McGraw-Hill, 2000). It is a right-brain guide to creating a family atmosphere in which love can thrive.

The author of numerous newspaper and magazine articles, Kuczmarski holds a Doctorate in Education and two master's degrees from Columbia

University in New York City, where she was named an International Fellow and a Fellow of the School of International and Public Affairs (SIPA). She has a B.A. from Colorado College, where she has returned to teach leadership. A lively radio and television guest, she has appeared on the *Today Show* and is widely quoted in print, including *Fast Company*, *The Wall Street Journal*, *Investor's Business Daily*, and *CNN Money*. She has been listed in the *Who's Who in the World* for 12 years, and included in *Outstanding People of the 21st Century*, *500 Leaders of World Influence*, *2000 Outstanding Writers of the 20th Century*, *Great Minds of the 21st Century*, and *International Who's Who of Professional and Business Women*.

She speaks on the topic of leadership around the world and on issues devoted to the contemporary family. Her research, writing, books, speeches, seminars, teaching, and innovation consulting have made her one of the top experts in the fields of leadership and family.

Thomas D. Kuczmarski is president and founder of the global consulting firm Kuczmarski Innovation and an internationally

recognized expert on innovation. Over the course of his career he has helped hundreds of clients, ranging from small businesses to Fortune 100 corporations, learn to systematically unlock the value of innovation. Mr. Kuczmarski teaches product and service innovation at Northwestern University's Kellogg Graduate School of Management where he is Senior Lecturer and Visiting Scholar in the Center for Innovation and Technology. For more than three and a half decades, his executive education courses at the Kellogg School have attracted leaders from around the world.

Mr. Kuczmarski is co-founder with journalist Dan Miller, of the Chicago Innovation Awards, which annually celebrates, educates, and connects innovators in the Chicago region. The awards are endorsed by every major business association in the Chicago region and showcase the creative spirit of America's heartland. In 2013, the Innovation Awards expanded to include a new venture, the Innovators Connection, designed to help expand the local economy by creating business connections among the region's innovators, large and small; in 2015, the Women's Mentoring Coop was created to foster mentoring relationships between women; and in 2016, the Chicago Student Invention Convention was added to enable elementary school students to learn about innovation.

Mr. Kuczmarski is the author of seven books on innovation and leadership. *Innovating Chicago Style: How Local Innovators are Building the National Economy* (Book Ends Publishing, 2012), written with Dan Miller and Luke Tanen, profiles the first decade of winners of the Chicago Innovation Awards and the lessons of innovation that they reveal. *Apples Are Square: Thinking Differently about Leadership* (Kaplan, 2007), co-authored with Dr. Susan Smith Kuczmarski, explores the qualities of the ideal leader and how to build those qualities into one's own career. *Innovating the Corporation* (NTC/Contemporary Publishing Group, 2001) reveals the seven steps for achieving growth through innovation. *Managing New Products* (Book Ends Publishing, 2000), now in its third edition, is endorsed by the American Marketing Association and widely regarded as one of the most comprehensive treatises on the development of new products. *Values-Based Leadership: Rebuilding Employee Commitment, Productivity and Performance* (Prentice-Hall, 1995) provided the first comprehensive treatise on values and norms in the corporation. In 1996, *Innovation* was co-published by NTC/Contemporary Publishing Group and the American Marketing Association.

He is extensively published and cited on radio, television, and in national periodicals including *The Wall Street Journal, Fortune,*

Newsweek, Bloomberg Business Week, The Today Show, Planning Review, Investor's Business Daily, USA Today, Marketing News, Advertising Age, Crain's Chicago Business, Business Marketing, the *Chicago Sun-Times*, the *Chicago Tribune*, and many more.

Mr. Kuczmarski is a highly regarded speaker on innovation management and leadership, and lectures nationally and internationally to a broad range of corporations and associations. He is Chairman of the advisory board of Chicago Innovation, trustee of the Retirement Research Foundation, board member of the Chicago Inventors Organization, a member of the Economic Club of Chicago, and an advisory board member of Blue Plate Catering.

Before founding Kuczmarski Innovation, he was a Principal at Booz Allen & Hamilton. While there, Mr. Kuczmarski assisted more than 100 U.S. consumer and industrial goods companies in the areas of marketing, new product development, strategic business analysis and organizational planning. In addition, he led the firm's in-depth research of the best practices employed by more than 700 U.S. firms in their new product management processes. His prior experience as a brand manager at Quaker Oats Company provided a solid and broad-based foundation unique to his consulting specialty.

He earned an M.B.A. from Columbia University's Graduate School of Business, and holds a master's degree in international affairs from Columbia University's Graduate School of International and Public Affairs, where he was named an International Fellow of the University. He received a B.A. in French from the College of the Holy Cross.

***

Married for over four decades, partners in life, Susan and Tom live in Chicago and are the parents of three adult sons.

To get information about consulting, seminars, teaching and speeches, contact the authors at www.kuczmarski.com.

ACKNOWLEDGMENTS

"The way to do fieldwork is to never come up for air until it is all over," advised Margaret Mead. Looking ahead, we have finally arrived at this point—and can now breathe! Looking back, we are especially grateful to those who have helped us along the way.

To Beth Ylvisaker, who lent her kind and generous ear and creative insight at many points in the lengthy writing process, we extend our gratitude for her friendship and guidance.

To our dear friend, Martha Donovan (aka "Aunt Muppie"), who has lifted us up and shared life's turning points for forty years.

To Jacob Sherman, we applaud and thank him for his support and keen editing eye.

To all those individuals that we interviewed, whose personal reflections and stories we shared, we are deeply appreciative. These include David Ahrens, Brian Bannon, Mary Catherine Bateson, Jennifer Bentz, Carol Bernick, John Berschied, Orla Branigan, Sonny Garg, Virginia Duncan Gilmore, Chris Gladwin, Margaret Heater, Adam Hecktman, Dipak Jain, Kevin Jennings, Pete Kadens, Sandee Kastrul, Gerry Kern, Ryan Kunkel, Kristi Lafleur, Linda Mallers, Harper Reed, Joe Reynolds, Jack Riopelle, Marc Shiffman, Barbara Slater, Jeff Semenchuk, John Stroud, Mary Ellen Weber, and Sam Yagan. For each of you, we express our admiration and praise.

FOREWORD
WHERE WE BEGIN

"There is no exercise better for the heart than reaching down and lifting people up."
John Andrew Holmes, American politician, 1773-1843

Lifting People Up, our third book on leadership, completes our long-awaited trilogy of books aimed at reframing the way we think about leadership and people management. Our belief is that leaders need to embrace values and norms, adopt a new leadership archetype, and use praise and recognition to motivate employees.

In our first leadership book, *Values-Based Leadership* (1995), we discussed how the culture of the workplace cannot remain productive without shared values and norms. They serve to connect or join employees and management together. To be meaningful, all employees and managers must generate and agree upon values as a whole. Management, no matter how reasonable they might be, cannot simply hand down or mandate a set of values and norms. Suspecting that something was wrong with the culture of the American workplace, we conducted interviews with more than 200 employees in a variety of organizations. We found a major disconnect between the values described by people at the top of an organization and the ones described by people below. It was clear to us that many organizations had what we called a "values gap." We saw the need to instill a new vision within organizations and reinvigorate their heart and soul. Bringing back and prioritizing values and norms in organizations was, in part, our solution.

In our second leadership book, *Apples Are Square: Thinking Differently About Leadership* (2007), we profiled 25 highly effective men and women who created a new model of leadership by reshaping the workplace in unexpected ways. Collaborators, as opposed to controllers, these pioneers were "square apples." We presented a process for rejuvenating the workplace by mastering the six essential qualities of this new form of leadership: humility, compassion, transparency, inclusiveness, collaboration and values-based decisiveness. We detailed how to inspire others through communication, build strong relationships, create loyalty and retain employees, and encourage personal risk-taking, creativity and flexibility.

Our third leadership book, *Lifting People Up: The Power of Recognition* (2018), begins where the last one left off. In fact, this newest book's title was the last chapter in *Apples Are Square*. This intellectual "baton pass" allows us to move into a more focused discussion of the nuances and necessity of praise and recognition as a key factor in good people management. As detailed in *Apples Are Square*, humility and compassion are essential qualities of values-based leaders. Their relation to praise and recognition is perhaps best expressed by our friend and colleague, Dipak Jain, the former Dean of the Kellogg School of Management. We met Dipak nearly 30 years ago when he was a professor teaching at the university. In his characteristically gentle tone, he captures the true essence of humility. "There is an analogy I like involving fruit," said Jain. "The riper the fruit gets on a tree, it starts bending down towards the earth. As you go up in work and in life, you need to become more humble and more down to earth. You need to point more toward the earth than toward the sky." Indeed, the earth is what grounds us, provides stability, and because of gravity, keeps us upright. The same holds true for humility.

A marketing expert trained in mathematics and statistics, Jain assumed leadership of Kellogg in 2001 after serving for five years as the school's associate dean. Under his guidance and leadership, Kellogg was voted "Best Business School" a record five consecutive times in *Business Week's* survey of U.S. business schools. After 13 years in the Dean's office, Jain left to become Dean of INSEAD, one of the world's leading business schools with campuses in France, Singapore and Abu Dhabi. He then served as Director of the Sasin Graduate Institute of Business Administration at Chulalongkorn University in Bangkok.

He boasts a remarkable professional history, one that might breed a sense of superiority, but quite the opposite is true. Introspective and humble, often greeting others with a hug, Jain believes the key to leadership is to view others as working *with* you and not *for* you. When leaders or executives lack humility or consider themselves above other employees, they create inherent conflict within the organization. They limit resources available, and in doing so, limit the amount that the team as a whole is able to achieve. "I personally don't believe in a hierarchical system," said Jain. "Just because you are in a higher position at a company does not mean that others in a lower position should be viewed beneath you. I believe that heights were made to be looked at – not to be looked down from. When you reach a height, it is not time to look down upon others. Let others look up at you and see how they can also reach up."

Effective leaders take this to the ultimate—they lift people up. "I strongly believe that when you work with people you need to know how to lift them up," said Jain. "You need to create an environment where people feel that you really do inspire and lift them to a higher level. In turn, they should feel good working with you because they know they will be valued. They will also have an opportunity to move up – professionally, personally and emotionally. The whole concept of an environment that lifts people up is very important. It lets those around you see that working together helps everyone rise together, and that is where you develop a sense of inclusiveness with your people."

We totally agree with the mindset and methodology that Jain described, and made it our goal to find out more about techniques being used by values-driven leaders to lift up their employees. To explore this topic, we interviewed 30 experienced, highly accomplished, thought-inspiring leaders from a diverse mix of fields and backgrounds. Many of these people-focused leaders shared perspectives and beliefs on culture and leadership. We selected each interviewee not for their current position but rather for the depth and richness of their ideas. The collection of thoughts from the people we interviewed are used to provide real-world examples that we intersperse throughout the book.

As we will discuss, many emerging organizations have evolved to an asset-less state—at least in terms of traditional brick and mortar type assets. Organizations like Uber, Facebook and Airbnb grew to become multi-billion dollar companies without ownership of vehicles, plants, content or properties. Today, we have migrated from a manufacturing plant and equipment asset base to a shared-economy that is grounded in intellectual capital—which of course comes from people.

While people have become our predominate and most valuable asset, an organization's balance sheet still doesn't reflect this shift nor in any way quantify the economic worth of people. Accountants going forward will need to become unstuck in the past and soon recognize the need to add "peoplequity" to the balance sheet. There should be a new data-driven formula that creates an economic value for an organization's key asset—its people.

Let's begin.

INTRODUCTION – OUR PERSPECTIVE ON LEADERSHIP

"You never change things by fighting the existing reality. To change something, build a new model that makes the existing model obsolete."

Buckminster Fuller, inventor and futurist, best known for popularizing the geodesic dome

We have been exploring and researching the topic of leadership for the past twenty-five years. Every time we talk to people about it, observe it and engage in more research, some new aspect of leadership begins to unfold. Our newest focus is peopleship—getting the most from others *and* giving the most to them. How can we get the people we work with to contribute *at the highest possible level* to any conversation, cause or company? How can they feel valued, recognized and emotionally motivated?

Our Seven Core Beliefs

In this continued pursuit, we have identified seven core tenets that we believe in, embrace and endorse. Developed from our passion for the topic of leadership and our past research, seminars, teaching and consulting, they represent our own perspectives for making teams and organizations great.

First, shared values and norms are the DNA of a culture and serve as its compass. An effective leader models these core beliefs and behaviors.

At the heart of an organization's culture are its values and norms. How effectively a leader nurtures and models these core beliefs and behaviors determines the buy-in and adoption of them by others.

A shared set of values and norms serves to connect employees and management together. The best approach is to have everyone participate in generating and agreeing upon a common set of values. They simply can't be handed down from senior management, no matter how reasonable and fair they might be. Everyone has to be part of the process.

As values guide the culture, the "proof" that it is working is found in energized and happy people who create a shared culture that enriches their work lives. The people-focused process begins with a workplace that is meaningful and gratifying. Leaders must nurture a highly productive group of individuals who have a genuine sense of their own value, strong relationships with each other and a group identity. They know they are appreciated members of a common community. The workplace is propelled by the power and energy of a shared spirit and inspiring culture.

Second, great leaders reach out and serve others.

The road to success has as much to do with others as it does with you. A reach out and serve others mindset says, "let me try to make the workplace a better place." It can be as simple as getting someone some coffee or helping less experienced or younger co-workers with a problem. You might ask: "what does reaching out to others have to do with individual and organizational success?" A service-oriented mindset creates an open, giving and collaborative attitude and culture. By any standards, these qualities produce happier individuals and a more productive work environment. Giving to others magnifies our hearts in ways that loosen us up to better communicate, interact with and understand others. This has a profound impact.

When we give time, dollars, expertise, ideas, advice and sheer brawn, we create a giving environment. It is an environment that is not self-centered, and one that is intended to serve consumers and employees first. Within the business world one often hears, "The purpose of a corporation is to increase shareholder wealth." This is wrong! We strongly feel that the purpose of a corporation should be to create products, services and offerings that satisfy consumer and customer needs in a way that enables employees to feel proud of where they work, give back to their communities and as a result, reward shareholders with profits and increased stock price. The focus here is on the value of goods and services produced instead of the amount of the profits made.

The new mantra is: leave a legacy of service. Make giving a major part of your focus. Use your gifts — personal and professional — to enrich your relationships, job, team, organization and community. Make a substantial difference and do as much as you can for others. And encourage others to do the same. This is how improvement occurs. When we help others find ways to be of service to coworkers and the larger organization, we help them see the value of dedicating a portion of their lives to a larger purpose. Acts of kindness and service always help the giver as well as the receiver.

On the work front, make an effort to show kindness to your colleagues. Be aware of how kind coworkers are to each other. Try discussing with others what it means to be kind. Look for ways to show kindness to another person who may be especially needy – someone who has received bad news or is troubled. Talk to other team members to discover who may need a kind thought or act. How about the person who is "different?" How about the colleague who is difficult or mean? Even if one does not feel like reaching out, there is value in doing so because the act of serving others serves ourselves as well.

> **Third, the best leaders convey compassion and create partnerships, relationships and trust.**

Compassion is having a concern for the well-being of others. The word itself is from the Latin *cum patior*, to suffer with. It means understanding another person to such a degree that you can empathize entirely with their feelings and thoughts. A compassionate leader is gracious, pleasant, generous and non-judgmental — not the common characteristics that you would find in many corporate leaders today. But that is the whole point. We have all come to believe that a role model is a person who is strong-willed, determined, emotionless and firm. Yet, employees and customers feel far more comfortable with leaders who convey flexibility rather than rigidity. A leader needs to believe that these "softer" qualities are not signs of weakness, but sources of strengths.

Through empathy, compassionate leaders excel at finding the common links among people. They help discover their overlapping interests and intentions, as well as create new goals and objectives that all team members share. Finding common ground must be done diligently and consistently. It is very easy to take the path of least resistance — that is, to simply mandate what needs to be done. It is a far different thing to create a path that leverages everyone's strengths, makes everyone a part of the solution and enables them to function as a well-oiled machine.

When co-workers spend time finding common ground, they are far more able and willing to see leaders as facilitators and peers. They know how to listen deeply and care profoundly. Group members not only help each other answer the questions, "who am I," and "what are my needs," but also focus on "who are we" and "what are our needs?" Rather than just follow a leader, the people now lead themselves.

When a group establishes common bonds and really "clicks," the result can be an incredible pool of skills, knowledge, expertise and experience. Most leaders do not take advantage of this power source.

Have you sought an answer to a difficult question that has been troubling you from your co-workers? What comes back can be phenomenal! This collective thinking surfaces ideas of all kinds. Brainstorming is a powerful tool. When a group of caring individuals gets involved, one member can serve as a catalyst for another.

Using the collective knowledge of the group is a formidable skill that more leaders should engage in. Instead, all too often we see them hiding out in their office. They are afraid to admit that they don't know the answer to a question. That would make them appear weak and unknowledgeable to their employees, right? Aren't leaders supposed to have all the solutions? No, they're not! If leaders would open their doors, express their vulnerabilities and say to their group, "Let's solve this difficult problem together," they would receive better results from everyone.

> **Fourth, effective leaders build people up, cheer them on and root for others.**

Good leaders know that it's critical to keep the team open to new ideas, convey warmth and interest, identify and address members' needs, and apply knowledge to help them grow, rally together and cheer for others. They root for people.

More than any other factor, the boss determines the culture of the workplace. Many bosses are command-and-control types. Their organizations, for better or worse, follow controlled objectives. Check out your boss. If he or she has the following characteristics, then you work for a "control guy": gives orders, disciplines, likes hierarchy, has or wants all the answers, demands respect, obsesses about the bottom-line, focuses on limits, issues action-plans, is strict and constantly keeps employees in fear.

Now, consider another kind of boss; he or she roots for others, uses praise to encourage and accomplish tasks, and creates an environment where employees strive to perform at optimal levels not out of fear, but in the pursuit of personal development and shared success with the rest of their organization. The following list will help identify the traits of this facilitate-and-cheer boss: empowers, serves as a role-model, acts as an agent for change, connects or networks, facilitates, rewards, encourages speaking out, motivates, nurtures creativity, seeks vision, relates salary and bonus to performance, uses a teaching and rooting-for archetype, encourages mentoring, nourishes growth, asks questions and reaches out.

Bosses usually fit into one of these two categories. The command-and-control boss rarely praises people. The cheering boss is flexible, personal, finds time for others and *always* roots for people. This boss wants employees to reach their full potential, become the best that they can be and build a caring team.

Effective and caring leaders share a far-reaching effort to root for people—all the time and at every turn. There is no divided effort here; their love of people authentically permeates their work. They look out for others and are encouraging, advancing and promoting. One leader may be an advocate for women, ordinary people, the forgotten, unpopular causes or co-workers who lack prestige and clout to lobby on their own. Another leader may try to understand and respect different viewpoints, strive to align individual and team interests, embrace diversity, build on individual strengths and want to touch and improve the lives of others.

Fifth, great leaders recognize achievements, praise often and reward frequently.

Praise, rewards and recognition are powerful tools to teach, inspire and motivate, however each is terribly underused in the culture of the workplace. Teachers and parents give recognition and positive feedback to children all the time–isn't it peculiar that we seem to have omitted it from our work settings as adults? Over a lifetime, we spend as much time – often more –at work as we do at homes and in school. When we tell our children, "You've done a great job," their faces light up, and when they send back a smile, they reward us for our recognition. Work settings must do the same for employees. Providing recognition is as rewarding to the giver as it is to the receiver. After a while, giving recognition becomes as self-satisfying as receiving it.

A verbal thank you, of course, is the easiest and quickest recognition to give. When was the last time you wrote a brief note thanking the people who helped you with an assignment? Try it some time, and be sure to describe what they did particularly well. Maybe they will even write one to you, expressing gratitude for the opportunity to work with you.

A major shortfall is when employees don't send a "thank you" to the people they work with—or work for. For some odd reason, they don't think that it is their role. We have wrongfully been conditioned into thinking that praise and "thank you" come from the top down instead of the bottom up. But think of the positive impact on multiple people providing recognition to others at multiple levels within the organization, including people at the very top.

In addition, we need to have all employees understand the value and importance of tangible thank you notes, emails, cards and texts. The communication "vehicle" doesn't really matter although a card or email can be more expressive. The point is to thank a co-worker or manager if they take you out to dinner, give you a gift or provide you with a unique opportunity. Without a thank you, the person may inaccurately assume that you didn't really value the event, or worse yet, didn't appreciate what was done for you. And co-workers or managers most likely won't do it again!

Recognition is different from providing feedback to an individual. Recognition personally conveys a sense of appreciation and continued encouragement for a task or job performed well. It's fine for the focus of recognition to be the completed task, but for recognition to provide maximum benefit, it's important to have the individual feel greater self-worth—not just satisfaction about the action being recognized.

Recognition can be offered in a variety of ways and under different circumstances. It can be given for an employee's insight into identifying a problem, acknowledging the difficulties the employee encountered while solving the problem or understanding the benefits of the employee's solution. Providing positive reinforcement to employees along the way is far more motivating than waiting until the task has been accomplished.

An effective leader always seeks ways to provide recognition, yet so often we woefully under-recognize others. We hear managers lament, "But, you don't want to make people feel overconfident or think they're too good, because then they'll be asking you for more money." How naïve! When it's genuine and legitimate, recognition doesn't cause ego-inflation; rather, it strengthens an individual's inner core. It enables them to feel better about themselves and in turn perform more effectively and efficiently. When people are filled with self-doubt and question themselves, they under-perform. Their concentration becomes fragmented because they spend time and energy wondering if they are doing the right thing or if their efforts will be recognized.

Team or group leaders need to give far more thought into effective ways to provide their team members with recognition. At the same time, group members also have a responsibility to provide their leaders with positive recognition and reinforcement. Most people expect the flow of recognition to stem from the top down. How often have you complimented your boss for a job well done? Probably not often. And yet, providing recognition to those at the top can be enabling and motivating for them. Providing frequent recognition is beneficial because it leaves groups stronger, more confident and better motivated to perform productively and focus on the tasks at hand rather than worrisome self-doubt.

Sixth, successful leaders emphasize the strengths of others and communicate them regularly.

Effective peopleship leaders invest in human development, touch others and create connections with people. They recognize that it's best to build on people's strengths, not their weaknesses. Jack Riopelle, former chairman of Wisconsin Film & Bag, underscored: "My biggest measurement for success is whether or not I have accomplished what I believe to be my mission in business and personal life, and that is: did I really make others' lives better? And not just monetarily, did I make them feel better about themselves? Did I make them feel like they were capable of achieving more than they ever thought they could? If there are a number of people who attribute that to me, then I would have to say that I am successful."

With finite financial and capital resources, organizations are forced to make difficult choices with their investments. Businesses are always looking at ways to cut costs, increase productivity and improve efficiency. However, organizations would often be better served developing the incredibly valuable resource they already possess, a resource that is consistently under-utilized: their people. An investment in human development is critical.

"The organizations that have a better chance of staying together are the organizations that have an ongoing practice of human development taking place, so that individuals recognize that even if they stay in the same position, they have a chance to grow inside that position," Riopelle said. "And part of that is inspiring, nurturing and cultivating individual strengths and talents. You need development to do that. It's one thing for a leader to verbalize that, but it's another to put words into actions by creating an atmosphere where development is real."

Riopelle understands that empowering employees can have tangible benefits. When leaders motivate those around them, it pays dividends in terms of increased productivity and efficiency. Workers need to know that they are valued; people want to hear that they are capable of greatness.

"I hope that I inspire people by convincing them that they are capable of far more than they thought they were," Riopelle said. "As I say to my employees, as often as I can, 'It's not where you're from that counts, it's who you are inside as a person that counts.' And just because you're from a small town, just because you're from a poor family, just because you're from a dysfunctional family, just because you didn't go to the right school, whatever the perceived barrier is, it doesn't matter where you're from. It matters who you are. And if you focus on who you are and not where you're from, you have a better chance of getting individuals to see that they can compete, that they can grow, that they can take on more than they ever thought they could. And I think that's what a leader needs to do." We would define this as a "pluralistic mindset." That is, accepting people for who they are regardless of their born differences—which we also strongly believe in.

> *Seventh, great leaders are self-aware, understand who they are and help others discover and nurture their own leadership qualities.*

Reaching out and connecting with another person has a profound impact. It nurtures a deeper relationship, acknowledges the strengths inside and initiates a focus on others. A leader must balance the desire to respect the individuals of his team with the need to garner the greatest collective result. We believe that the individual is what the group is all about. The individual is the microcosm of the group; their collective energy comes from each individual.

To ignore the individual is to forget the unique talent everyone possesses. A leader that only looks at the collective whole is limited to noticing only the similarities between individuals. Shared Kevin Jennings, a Manhattan-based personal counselor: "If you put your focus on the group, it often means that you are going to speak to the level of the least common denominator, whereas if you address the individual, you unlock the extraordinary and you begin to access the group's unique resources."

We have convinced ourselves that success is reaching some arbitrary bar set by others, but we rarely accept that the most important bar is the one we set for ourselves. "I want people to understand that developing and cultivating the self is the key to happiness," Jennings said. "I think part of the problem in the world today is that people are almost relentlessly externally focused. We are taught by and indoctrinated with images and bombarded by other people's philosophies. If the value of the self and the understanding that happiness and the pursuit of happiness are the same as the pursuit of self-realization, then people can take root in themselves. As they take root in the substance of their own being, they are better able to discern, in a sense turn off the outside images, and open more within so that a kind of balance or harmony is restored."

Money, titles and pictures on the front pages of newspapers are symbols of what people think success must look like. Instead, Jennings recognizes that joy and success come from knowing ourselves. That type of happiness does not require riches.

Leaders can help others reach self-realization and find themselves. In today's fast-paced, competition-filled, media-saturated world, the seemingly simple ideal of self-realization seems hidden under a cloud of confusion. Future leaders must work to create environments where individuals feel comfortable turning inward.

Our seven core beliefs, we believe, help create an environment where people feel valued, contribute to the advancement of their organization and collaborate in a synergistic way. We feel there is a need to define a new mindset and leadership style—which we call "peopleship"—and have created a set of six tools and techniques for activating it. But before we can activate these tools to lift people up in our organizations, we have to truly understand the basic tenants of this new peopleship mindset.

Our core leadership beliefs that build people value are:

- *Values and norms are the DNA of a culture and serve as its compass.*

- *Great leaders reach out and serve others.*

- *The best leaders convey compassion and create partnerships, relationships and trust.*

- *Effective leaders build people up, cheer them on and root for others.*

- *Great leaders recognize achievements, praise often and reward frequently.*

- *Successful leaders emphasize the strengths of others and communicate them regularly.*

- *Great leaders are self-aware, understand who they are and help others discover and nurture their own leadership qualities.*

SECTION

1

LIFT UP

CHAPTER 1
THE NEW WAY—
PEOPLESHIP

"Take away my people, but leave my factories and soon grass will grow on the factory floors. Take away my factories, but leave my people and soon we will have a new and better factory."

Andrew Carnegie, industrialist and philanthropist

The future will be marked by innovative organizations trying to improve results through people. Attracting and retaining the most talented people, getting their best thinking and enabling their collaboration will bring profound results to organizations. This "people business" is the next frontier.

People offer a new source of competitive advantage. In the past, organizations would create a strategy around cost-reductions, market differentiation or innovation. While these strategies should still exist, the new paradigm is to work with the people within organizations to achieve their fullest potential.

We have seen it all so far—from reengineering and restructuring to retooling and reorganizing! The next phase, finally, calls for a focus on people. We call this new approach or new organizational lens, "people-ship." It is a new mindset for leading a team or an entire organization.

Peopleship is a new form of leadership that will enable organizations to achieve unprecedented levels of higher performance. It shifts the attention onto the people rather than the leader at the top. This new leadership approach can also give organizations an innovative edge. Propelled by the power and energy of a shared spirit and innovative culture, organizations can navigate successfully in a challenging, competitive and changing world. This "business of people" can revolutionize management and leadership.

In an organization driven by peopleship, the culture of the workplace is completely different. Individuals work in an environment in which they can more effectively free up their thinking and work together more constructively, creatively and gainfully.

What Is Peopleship?

Peopleship is the leadership mentality of motivating people to lead themselves rather than dutifully following a superior. Intrinsic motivators and self-directed work teams drive individuals. The workplace develops individuals who listen intently and exert their maximum effort and energy toward realizing collaborative goals. Peopleship energizes and enables individuals within organizations to build strong relationships, enhance their self-worth, shine outward, draw and develop their potential to the maximum, and believe in the collective goals and values established by the group. A peopleship organization creates a deep connection between and among its members. Together, they are fortified to embrace risk and innovation, explore uncharted waters and discover new territory.

Hopefully, "peopleship" will soon become a new word found in *Webster's Dictionary*.

---

peopleship ('pēpəl 'SHip) noun

- a leadership approach focused on cultivating and motivating people
- a management style activated by six leadership tools—listen, include, free, trust, use rewards, and praise
- a technique to help people unleash their inner leader
- a process to build a high-performing culture from the ground up

---

Peopleship—versus leadership—is a new management practice that gets the most out of people and gives them the most in return.

Peopleship encourages working together, side-by-side in teams on what really matters—that is, the shared goals, mission and values of an organization that build a strong sense of community. In turn, their shared values are reinforced by norms and behaviors.

Self-motivation and self-directed work streams prevail in a peopleship culture. Emphasis is placed on developing individuals in a way that gives each a trusted relationship, which enables more independence on one hand yet greater collaboration on the other. Peopleship energizes and empowers individuals. Team members are participative, supportive, equal in status, respectful of individual opinions and group decisions, and agree upon common goals. Peopleship creates a deep connection among committed individuals.

By "lifting people up," we are better able to develop, enhance and connect employees and managers in an optimal way. Working together side-by-side to do something that matters, even in unfavorable conditions, builds a sense of unity and community. Most people want to be part of something where they truly believe their impact can make a positive difference. They want to feel valued by peers and managers within an organization. When people feel and know that they are valued and make a significant impact on an organization, they routinely strive to not only perform at peak levels, but also improve their skills so they can make a greater difference in the future. Thus, successful organizations are communities with leaders who lift people up to meet their full potential. After all, doesn't almost everyone want to improve and make their team or world better? These leaders are *mindful*, *collaborative* and *excited to give recognition*. Indeed, they acknowledge the benefit of lifting people up—not knocking them down. Peopleship leaders embrace these six habits:

L for Listen

I for Include

F for Free

T for Trust

U for Use Rewards

P for Praise

The future of our organizations depends upon our collective ability to get both people management and motivation right. As more intellectual capital, specialized training, advanced technology applications and higher expertise-based jobs emerge, we will need to develop and advance our people more than ever. Our ability to manage them better than our competitor will be the source of our future innovative edge.

The "Big Picture" Objectives

While it will take considerable time to nurture our six leadership habits in leaders and team members, it is well worth the investment. Going forward, success takes on a different meaning. People's performance rather than financial performance is the number one criterion of success. Financial performance is still important of course, but our focal lens shifts such that we see revenues and profits as the result of getting optimal performance from our people. If we put our care and attention toward them, the money will follow.

We believe there are specific ways to transform the workplace. We need to pay attention to both individuals *and* teams. If we successfully energize each, the result will be a growing and committed organization. By being self-reflective and leveraging values supported by defined norms or behaviors, we are able to build strong and effective relationships and teams within an organization. Ultimately, we hope that future people-centric organizations will:

- Foster a culture of *innovation* and *shared leadership*.
- Create a *small start-up mindset* within a large organization.
- Allow more thinking-time and *self-renewal* for individuals.
- Spread *leaders throughout the organization*—not group them at the top.

- *Pay people on performance*, not tenure nor title.

- Nurture *self-discovery*, *collaboration* and *recognition*.

A "lifting people up" leader creates a committed, high-performance culture—one that yields both short-term results *and* longer term benefits. Our new leadership concept has a transformational capability. If we are able to more successfully leverage our highest-potential assets—our people—our return on investment could grow exponentially.

Peopleship is a new form of leadership that motivates and cultivates the people within the organization. It is marked by six leadership habits or qualities to "lift up" others: Listen, Include, Free, Trust, Use Rewards, and Praise.

CHAPTER 2
BRIDGING THE PEOPLE DIVIDE

"At first people refuse to believe that a strange new thing can be done, and then they begin to hope it can be done, then they see it can be done—then it is done and all the world wonders why it was not done centuries ago."

Frances Hodgson Burnett, author, *The Secret Garden*

Organizations accomplish what individuals cannot, yet individuals are the heart and soul of every team or organization. Undeniably, it is the contributions of these individuals—their talents, hopes and insights—that create the workplace. Importantly, these individuals need to be recognized. They need to believe that what they are doing is valued and appreciated by others. Working together in teams, people can leverage their strengths, make significant contributions even in the midst of difficult conditions, and over time build a sense of community, shared spirit and culture.

Brian Bannon, Commissioner and CEO of the Chicago Public Libraries, shared with us his perspective on the importance of libraries, stressing how they need to evolve with the changing trends and technologies of how information is consumed. He too believes that great organizations stem from the effective collaboration of a team of people.

"Libraries have long been the cornerstone for the public's right to information and knowledge. However, as technology expands with the arrival of the digital age, the question has been asked, 'do we still need libraries?'" His answer was a fervent one: "Long ago and still today, we need a place to connect people and ideas in order to make a stronger, more democratic society. This mission really hasn't changed. When I think about the Chicago Public Library, we have to be clear. We are here, of course, because we have an education agenda. But the library's essence is also about how we leverage the power of libraries to make our communities stronger and more connected. *'How do we bring people together to collaborate?'* "

To provide some history, "Benjamin Franklin was instrumental in creating the first library. He believed that physical space was needed where a blacksmith and a surgeon could come together and discover and witness a demonstration of the leading 'technology' of the day. The library, then and now, is an informal space to support creativity and innovation—and foster collaboration." Though they were 240 years apart, both Benjamin Franklin and Brian Bannon were right on the mark. As true now as it was then, we need to foster a sense of collaboration and further build teams and communities.

A Focus on People

Our new leadership approach is focused on the inclusion, development, cultivation and recognition of people. We often hear, "people are the lifeblood of our organization!" Well, this new perspective finally reinforces that concept. Leadership is all about the people—not just one leader. Leadership *evolves* into peopleship. Our new leadership construct lets the people of an organization build the foundation and culture. With the focus placed on team members and their individual self-awareness and growth, people learn to lead themselves.

The Leadership Lens—A Triple Focus

What does the new lens of leadership look like? It has *three* distinct focal points:

1. Self-discovery and mindfulness
2. Collaboration and group connection
3. Praise and recognition

The test for the first, and most difficult to put in place, is: Do team members grow as individuals? Do they become stronger, wiser, freer and more creative? The test for the second is: Does the team or organization function smoothly and effectively? Does it become more inclusive, collaborative, committed and productive? The test for the third is: Is the right kind of praise and recognition given? How can we give praise to create people who are self-confident and high-performing individuals? How can we use rewards to build team member community, commitment and productivity?

The process of learning leadership requires *both* personal self-reflection and community building. It involves active individual engagement, personal conflict and self-awareness. At the same time, it is collectively experienced and shared; each person contributes to the organization's mission, values and cultural agenda. Focus must be placed *both* on the individual—to develop, engage and unleash abilities—and the team or organization—to define and reach its goals and bottom line. One can't live without the other. It's more than just the individual, and it's more than just the team. It's the two of them.

You might ask, "But how does this triple-focused leadership 'lens' differ from traditional leadership?" Traditional leadership focuses primarily on the leaders at the top, not the team members or followers. They put more effort into pleasing their boardrooms and shareholders then their employees. It also looks more at the charisma and personality traits that make an influential top-down leader. Good traditional leaders often use their believed-to-be inborn talents to control and compete; they influence or tell followers what to do, and triumph over whatever situation they confront. These hierarchical, bureaucratic, old-style leaders watch over and hand down directives "from above" and demand results.

We are wrongfully led to believe that leaders are born, not developed. A soccer player with average raw talent can become great by practicing hard, gaining experience and becoming an outstanding captain of the team. Another player may have innate skills that he or she was born with, but without leveraging them properly will never reach full potential. Of course, being born with these skills and working hard to hone them will result in the best leader possible. So, are leaders born or developed? Yes.

The Leader or the Pack?

Something else happens when these hierarchical structures are in place, as described here by Carol Bernick, former CEO of Alberto-Culver: "One of the biggest faults is too many people get to the top of whatever organization or division they're in, and they stop dealing with people. They isolate themselves in offices, they have their executive team, they sit in their meeting with ten people and they think they basically have the pulse of the organization. But really, they are missing *everything* about the pulse of the organization."

Dacher Keltner, in *How to Rise to the Top Without Losing the Virtues that Got You There,* cautions: "studies show that people in positions of corporate power are three times as likely as other employees to interrupt coworkers, raise their voices and say insulting things at the office." These characteristics only move people out the door to work at other companies or organizations. They depict the opposite of peopleship.

Our people-focused structure is vastly different. While still results-focused, it enables leaders to feel the "pulse" of the organization, nurture minimal hierarchy, share leadership, openly express ideas and put learning and personal growth top-of-mind. With self-awareness, both personal and through group discovery, serving as the engine, they are simply better places to live and work. You might ask, how can this be?

This is where values come in. Values are generated from within—from the bottom up, not from the top down. Mutually agreed-upon, values and norms serve as the steering wheel for the entire workplace. They link employees together without the need for bureaucratic rules and corporate regulations. The important point, and often one that is missed, is that everyone must be given an equal say in setting up and building the group's values.

One might ask: "What is the leader's job?" Our answer is to create a "values-ful" culture where leaders listen, include, free, trust, use rewards and praise.

A Democratic Community

A democratic community, what educational psychologist John Dewey called a community always "in the making," cannot exist without people, or what he called "live learners." A community is a network or circle of people, connected together on a project. The group of people values itself, sometimes even more than they value the project.

Peopleship enables individuals to use their talents to contribute individually or collaboratively. The cornerstone to our new model of leadership is just this – *individual participation*. It is key to everything. One must get involved, encourage others to get involved, and motivate and reward individual creativity, productivity and accomplishment. Individuals participate by getting engaged and making decisions within their own area of responsibility.

One consequence of peopleship is power-sharing. With people in charge of their own processes, they are able to assume accountability for themselves and share responsibilities with others in the workplace community. They become empowered leaders through their participatory actions at work.

The old model of leadership has the leader at the top keeping the power and making the decisions. Leaders were seen as superior. They gave and delegated responsibility, engaged in command and control behaviors, and led from above. In contrast, the rest of the organization received and accepted responsibility, followed orders, did imposed tasks and were led by others above.

This style of leadership is a vertical power structure, involving a relationship between those in high, middle and lower positions. Someone is leading and someone is led. It is an inherently authoritarian system where a person in a higher position is assigned authority to make decisions regarding those below.

In contrast, peopleship is founded on relationships between equals and peers. An interaction is carried out without rank or position. It is an egalitarian system. Dignity and mutual respect are the core values in shaping power relationships between people in the workplace. Everyone has independent and inter-responsible roles; it is a horizontal relationship. In fact, there are multiple leaders. All individuals lead in tandem with each other!

We believe this is a new way of doing business and a new way to harness trust in people. Without question, people are any organization's source of energy, creativity and emotional vibrancy.

Our leadership model is both practical and visionary. You will see that the emphasis on trusting and working with people is as important, if not more, than the emphasis on making money. The new bottom line is investing in the personal and professional growth of employees as a means of creating a financially-viable organization.

Having the best people and getting their very best thinking and creativity will profoundly improve organizations. Energized and motivated people, no doubt, can achieve great things in the workplace.

Imagine eliminating one or two tiered layers within your own organization. Employees and leaders end up working together more as equals—as partners. Each will bring different skills, forms of intelligence and contributions to the organization and no one will feel like a subordinate underneath someone else. Future organizations will readily recognize the positive energy and effectiveness of leading people differently.

Our new leadership has three focal points—self-discovery and mindfulness, collaboration and group connection, and praise and recognition. Lots of leaders are in place and power-sharing is their mantra.

CHAPTER 3
"L" FOR LISTEN

"When you talk, you are only repeating what you already know. But if you listen, you may learn something new."

The Dalai Lama, spiritual leader of the Tibetan people

There are six leadership habits that successful leaders tend to adopt that shape how they interact with others. The first habit is to compassionately "listen." Listening, both to one's self and to others, is a core component of mindfulness. It promotes self-discovery, while simultaneously enabling others to be heard, felt and valued. Listening is probably the *most* powerful leadership habit; it is essential to the core principles of peopleship.

Much to our fascination, there is a relationship between the concepts of listening and silence. In order to listen, one has to be silent. But people are often very uncomfortable with silence. One can observe this any time there is a pause in a conversation—it rarely takes longer than a few seconds of silence before someone jumps in to say something.

Perhaps this is one reason why we are (for the most part) poor listeners. We are afraid of silence and avoid it at all costs. Yet, when we look at the words "listen" and "silent," we discover that each is spelled with the exact same letters. You can't have one without the other. Examining the connection between the two concepts can give us powerful insight—we need to stop talking, accept silence and listen.

Lead by Listening

We recently went on a bird walk with a remarkable ornithological guide at our local botanic garden. At the beginning of the ninety-minute "class," the guide paused for thirty seconds of silence. Afterward she shared that she had heard the sounds of eight different kinds of birds during her short listening time. This was a shocker! We often miss out on sounds—and the information that comes from them—because of ambient noise. In this case, we didn't hear the crisp, clear and distinctive "chirps" because of moving cars, talking people and distracting gardeners nearby.

We have plenty of ambient noise and distraction in our workplace too. People are often not listening deeply, nor are they engaged in prolonged face-to-face conversation. They are often busy with emails, text messages and voicemail. Even personal phone conversations have radically declined. While digital technology allows us to communicate faster, we miss out on hearing a voice or feeling a person's emotions. The larger picture here: intimacy, empathy and identity are all developed from our one-to-one conversations, and all of that goes into building a community. So we are in an exceedingly troubling spot; our ability to listen actively and compassionately is diminishing.

The Roles of Speaker and Listener

The digital age brings challenges to having real-world and in-person conversations, or rather it facilitates avoiding them. As a consequence, we should be reminded of the special, and sometimes forgotten, roles of speaker and listener. The *listener* should observe the speaker attentively and express feelings of warmth, interest and enthusiasm. Physical contact, even smiles, also convey skillful listening. The *speaker* should observe the listener attentively, looking for these same indicators to assure she is listening. While it is the role of the speaker to communicate a specific message, it is the role of the listener to not only receive the words, but understand and analyze their meaning. Lastly, it's crucial that the listener acknowledges that the message has been received. This deep listening is rarely experienced anymore.

An active listener will communicate that they are with you in any number of ways. Their eyes are alert, they may nod their head, ask follow-up questions, verbally acknowledge that they have understood an idea or add information. If their posture is alert, they get closer to you physically, shut the door to outside noise or ask others to join the group, then you know the listener has been attentive.

Most speakers know whether or not active listening has occurred. To communicate this, perhaps we should abruptly *stop talking* when we discover that a person is not listening. "Why talk when no one seems to be listening?" Oddly, many adults will continue talking even when there are no signs that someone is listening! They have forgotten how to observe the listener.

Watching for indicators is not easy to do. If there are no questions or if eye contact is poor (e.g. looking out the window), then it should be clear to the speaker that two-way communication isn't happening. Good speakers know when someone isn't actively listening to them; they know their "audience" is not there to catch their thoughts.

Remember, the listener's main task is to understand what the speaker is trying to say and to let him or her know that they understand. Attitude is just as important as what you reply. In fact, nonverbal responses can often convey more meaningful and quicker feedback than words. Focus on and check your own listening skills. Ask yourself if you:

1. *Are being attentive.*

2. *Accept what the speaker is saying.*

3. *Are trying to understand and clarify.*

4. *See your own views changing.*

5. *Encourage the speaker.*

6. *Paraphrase what the speaker says.*

7. *Provide praise or positive reinforcement.*

If you follow these guidelines, you will not only listen more deeply, but also gain much more out of conversations.

Listen Deeply

We listened deeply when we were children. This is how we learned as infants, then as toddlers and young children. Unfortunately, when we become adults many of us stop hearing. We focus instead on talking about our own ideas and ourselves, all the while neither listening nor asking questions. We need to jump-start our deep listening abilities and recover this lost skill.

How do we renew and improve our deep listening? Practice, practice, practice. And ask other people questions! Virginia Gilmore, founder of the Sophia Foundation, did just this. Her perspective shares her ability to deeply listen: "Continual learning is really an energy generator for me, and I think it's also a practice. Because if you really practice dialogue, you hold your judgments aside and you listen to somebody else. I think the learning helps open me up to thinking differently."

The moment we stop learning is the moment that we stop listening. It is the moment in which we boast that we know enough and what we know is right. No individual can or should ever reach that point. Instead, we should cherish our opportunities to learn and grow.

"I value deep listening," Gilmore said, "which has probably been the most important capacity that I have been developing through dialogue and also my own spiritual practice, listening to my inner self, listening at a deep level to others and really hearing myself and others."

Sometimes we are so used to shutting people out that we need to train ourselves to listen. And there is so much out there to listen to: friends, family, colleagues, teachers and certainly our own hearts and minds. The more you listen, the clearer things become, and one critical way to do that is asking others questions. It conveys interest and signals that you want to listen—not just talk.

Give Others the Floor

The practice of giving others a voice is important in creating a positive and engaging culture. Leaders can create methods or forums that allow others to communicate their needs, problems and issues. This creates a sense of togetherness and a feeling that we are "heard" in the organization. Here are a few success stories that surfaced in our interviews that offer easy ways to listen to others:

- "We have a staff meeting every Tuesday and everyone has the floor. I manage it very entrepreneurially. I let others run the show." Linda Mallers of FarmLogix

- "We have healthy systems in place. We personally meet with every employee one-on-one several times a year. We have weekly manager meetings, monthly departmental 'wrap ups,' and company-wide 'wrap ups' for thirty minutes about the direction of the company, followed by dinner and happy hour." Joe Reynolds of Red Frog Events

- "Every week we have someone present a topic of their choice for five to seven minutes. They can't read from their notes, and they have to give compelling arguments." Pete Kadens, then at SoCore Energy

Giving employees a voice empowers individuals and teams, builds leadership skills and creates a collaborative culture. If you haven't yet done so, put a "forum" in place to ensure that team members have a chance to express themselves as well as listen. Whether through one-on-one sessions or regular larger group gatherings, open the lines of communication. When listening takes place and voices are heard, collaboration is nurtured, people feel valued, and two-way communication and contribution are set in motion. Listening actually inspires individuals to contribute and be an integrated part of the team.

Listen to the Self

We all need time for personal reflection. Virginia Duncan Gilmore, founder of the Sophia Foundation, decided to leave the fourth-generation family company she helped lead as she found herself in the middle of a divorce and watching her last child leave for college. Immobilized from these life changes, she knew she needed to listen to her "self." Everything was crashing down on her. As she put it, "I simply had to get off the merry-go-round. My inner needs were so strong at that point I just had to stop and deal with them." She took time off to reflect and get in touch with what she wanted to do next.

Personal reflection is crucial for developing greater *self-awareness*, one of our cornerstones of peopleship. High-five on this point: listening to the "self" leads to self-discovery! Here are a few ways to listen to your inner voice:

- Rise early, take a long walk and fuel the "self" with exercise, nature and reading.

- Reduce stress by reminding yourself you don't need to make everything perfect.

- Be present and positive.

- Catch the sunrise, take a swim or hike a mountain at some point during the week—just get outside!

- Find energy from spending meaningful time with family or a close friend.

- Use healthy food, music and travel to fuel renewal.

- Reach outwards to do some community service work.

- Simplify; get rid of clutter and switch gears.

Make a list of the things that complicate your life, then start to minimize and eliminate them. Concentrate on a *new list* of things that lead to more self-discovery. It will help to keep your energy level up, free up leisure time and make your career a constant source of joy.

When we simplify, not only do we have more energy but we become more creative. We become more free for personal growth. Every person needs to learn how to conserve energy when they can so they can release it when they choose. Simplify and shed. Your relationships will deepen and flourish, and to our point, you will be able to listen to the "self" inside you.

L = LISTEN. Sharing ideas and feelings develops meaningful relationships at work. Make use of the many opportunities to practice active listening, keep in mind the roles of listener and speaker, and take some time to listen to your "self" along the way.

CHAPTER 4
"I" FOR INCLUDE

"The capacity for relating one's self easily to other men and women is not inborn, but a result of experience and training, and that experience and training is itself social."

**George C. Homans, author of *The Human Group*
and founder of behavioral sociology**

To properly "lift people up," it's important to be mindful of inclusion. That means we accept people for who they are, and we start with a viewpoint that their strengths and differences are what we want to build-up and leverage. Leaders value each person and maintain the assumption that everyone has the potential to be a high-performing contributor—and they can! This sense of inclusiveness is a leadership characteristic that is often hard to come by, and things like diversity programs within organizations are only the first step. Securing a diverse mix of people is a good start, but true progress is made when managers make the effort to assure that these people feel included, valued and connected to the overall goals and mission of the organization.

We have uncovered three ways to help team members feel included and linked to the organization: (1) create a caring and inclusive community, (2) integrate individuals into teams and groups and (3) leverage mentoring as an inclusion method.

1. Create a caring and inclusive community.

We both had the incredibly rewarding experience of taking a graduate course with the well-respected anthropologist Margaret Mead at Columbia University in New York City. Her course was different from most. She exuded passion in every class she lectured, grading and commenting herself on each student's term paper. Unlike other professors, she didn't use a teaching assistant. She communicated that she cared about her students' learning and about her lessons and messages. She cultivated an inclusive attitude and caring classroom community — even at the age of seventy-two. Outside the classroom she was often seen walking on campus, distinguished by her tall English-made walking stick which became her trademark. She was usually accompanied by a small group of students deep in conversation, which perfectly exemplifies her efforts to nurture and cultivate a caring relationship with them.

As an anthropologist, she was exposed to scores of different cultures and a diverse mix of ethnic groups from around the world. We believe strongly, as she did, in the power of culture bound by a common set of values and norms. Mead observed that when groups of people were functioning optimally, they created a special caring and respect for one another in their culture.

Think about it. When you really know that someone cares for and about you, whether it's professional or personal, you respond to and behave differently with that person. Typically, you are more open, trusting and secure. In a caring and inclusive environment, individuals are motivated, committed and productive. This allows for more open and direct dialogue and communication, limits feelings of isolation and helps to build trust in the relationship. It's this caring, inclusive element that often distinguishes effective groups from massively dysfunctional ones.

Hundreds of social scientists have focused on the concept of community over the last fifty years. A community provides an internal feeling of purpose and sense of individual security. There are shared goals, values, missions and related activities. The community provides a strong sense of support for its members. If a supportive foundation is in place, members can take risks and experiment freely. Groups provide for their members' needs, interests and feelings. This is what inclusivity can breed in the workplace. It not only brings people together, it serves as a guideline for the way we interact with one another within our work settings. Our take-away: we should hire a diverse group of people of varying genders, races, ages and backgrounds in order for inclusivity to be genuine.

2. Integrate individuals into teams and groups.

How does one learn how to become a *member* of a particular team or organization? Employees need to feel attached, connected and part of the group. They need to know that they belong and that they play a critically important role in the growth of their organization. They need to be involved in shaping the culture in which they work.

Kristi Lafleur, the former CEO of the Illinois Tollway told us, "Culture is the collective vision for how people see themselves and how they act." We agree. Many times, culture means one thing to senior management and something very different to team members. Our research confirmed that unless norms and values are agreed upon, adopted and put in place within an organization, a "values gap" will widen between leaders and team members. Often, employees view culture as the environment created by top management. Organizational leaders, on the other hand, view culture as the way in which employees interact with one another. This illustrates the disconnect that exists between workers and management. We need to create teams and organizations with clear norms and values that provide a pattern for linking together all individuals, and ultimately blur the line between the traditional hierarchies and organizational "layers."

Cultural traditions, rituals and habits within a workplace often seem to originate with upper managers and leaders, but team members don't always recognize or accept management conclusions. Team members may not find value in these upper-management-driven traditions and attitudes. And why should they? The culture doesn't reflect the values or beliefs of the team members—only senior management's.

At other times, however, management sends mixed messages. When this happens, team members may choose to select certain things from the culture and adapt them differently, or they might cynically reject them altogether. The key is to integrate shared values and norms into an existing culture by translating past traditions into ones that provide meaning and benchmarks to guide behavior for current and future team members.

An effective culture caters to and builds upon the values of all team members. We need to encourage leaders and team members alike to see and understand how their organization's culture creates a sense of inclusiveness. By taking part in establishing their own cultural values and norms, they tightly weave themselves into the "cloth" of the organization. *The* organization becomes *their* organization.

3. Leverage mentoring as an inclusion method.

Mentoring is another way to integrate individuals into a team or organization. A mentor is a supporter of the individual — someone who provides the wisdom and expertise to help advance the individual's career and help resolve professional issues and problems. "I'm looking out for your best interests and I'm here to serve as a sounding board for you." This is the mindset of a good mentor. Mentors also serve to integrate team members into the culture. But in order for a mentoring relationship to really work well, a mutually agreed-upon partnership is essential. If a mentor is simply "assigned" to an employee, it usually won't work. A partnership should be built that is based on mutual trust and respect. It needs to evolve over time.

Mentors can act as any combination of an advisor, trainer, friend, counselor, sage, teacher, confidant and big sister/brother. Mentoring can provide powerful advancement of an individual's personal and professional development. When it is done well and a true partnership is created between two individuals, an employee feels more connected and integrated into the organization. It can also help to build a stronger sense of community within the workplace. How? Mentors provide a support system — they serve as both coach and cheerleader! They focus on helping an individual join a group and remain a cooperative member of that group.

It is *critically important* that mentoring programs exist within the workplace. However, they should be designed to be as flexible as possible, with the bulk of the relationship up to the mentor and mentee.

Lastly, those we talked with almost unilaterally stated that there was a need for this relationship to be both personal and professional.

We offer a few specific guidelines to achieve this. Get started with a two-hour meeting to discuss goals and objectives of the mentor-mentee relationship and what the roles of each should be. Follow-up this meeting with a written agreement between the two individuals on what those goals and objectives are. This agreement should then be submitted to someone in the workplace who will serve as the mentor's leader — an interested individual who will guide the mentors and focus on *mentor coaching*. The mentor leader is responsible for mentor-mentee selection, matching, relationship encouragement, check-in and suggested follow-up. There are a few "rules" each mentor-mentee should try to follow: schedule periodic get-togethers or chats to keep each other up-to-date, schedule a regular meal or drink to discuss personal and professional issues out of the office, and lastly develop a brief development plan. Time and attention placed on each of these initiatives helps build relationships that nourish and flourish.

I = INCLUDE. Team members feel included and connected when a caring and inclusive community is set in place. They can play a part in shaping the culture and supporting mentoring programs.

CHAPTER 5
"F" FOR FREE

"One does not discover new lands without consenting to lose sight of the shore for a very long time."

André Gide, French author and
Nobel Prize in Literature winner

For many, unfortunately, the notions of "work" and "freedom" are in direct contrast. When employees are unhappy with their work environments, they feel uninterested, unmotivated and unable to perform at their peak. They feel *trapped*. Leaders need to foster a more "free" mindset among their employees so they feel empowered to test their limits, and in so doing, create a culture of innovation and open-mindedness throughout the organization.

"Free" means to take an innovative and discovery-oriented approach to most every task or project. This is achieved by fostering a creative and open mindset. Let new ideas in and flourish. In order to achieve this, both sides of the brain need to be activated. It is important to integrate left and right brain thinking by nurturing individuals and teams to think logically *and* express emotion openly, freely and heartfully. Let creativity reign.

Leaders who convey "free" as the operative and desired state of mind at work will cultivate a group of people who embrace creativity, innovation, problem-solving and new ways of thinking.

We need employees and managers to feel that it is okay to fail. Without this mindset, people will not take risks, they won't think differently and they won't reach their full potential. People should be encouraged every day to explore new alternatives, try new things, innovate new approaches and programs, and look at everything from a different perspective. Ultimately, everyone within an organization should feel, be and act freely in order to optimize the power of their left and right brain potential.

Use Both Sides of the Brain

The brain has two halves, each with a different style of thinking and energy. The left brain is the know-it-all. It is the master of expressing itself logically, verbally and through the written word. It is analytical, rational, objective and detail-oriented as it focuses on each step in any process. The right side is sometimes called "the silent partner"; it expresses itself sporadically through rhythms, patterns and pictures. It cannot articulate itself in words. It is visual, intuitive, subjective and "big picture" oriented as it focuses on the interrelationships between the steps in any process. The left side is time centered and the right side is timeless. The left is linguistic, while the right is musical. The left aggressive, the right yielding.

Whole Brain Leadership

Betty Edwards, in her book *Drawing on the Right Side of the Brain,* shows us the power of using both sides of the brain. She believes that everyone can draw, even those who don't think they can. To prove this, she asks her students to draw a picture of Picasso's "Portrait of Igor Stravinsky." Then, she asks them to turn the Picasso portrait upside down and draw it again. When the students compare the two drawings, they find that the first attempt is quite poor, while the upside down version is rather good. Edwards offers the following explanation: "The left brain refused the task of processing the upside-down image. Presumably, the left hemisphere, confused and blocked by the unfamiliar image, turned off and the job passed over to the right hemisphere." The left brain is forced to admit that it performs better with the right brain than without it.

Teams and organizations often ignore this "whole-brained" way of thinking. Take a look at how-to books available to leaders. Most of them focus on the left brain aspect of leadership, or how to generate, evaluate and change behaviors. But leadership is a whole-brain activity. The energy of the left side says "take charge," while the energy of the right side says "flow." If we learn to balance these energies, what might happen to our work? We believe that this will lead to stronger relationships, greater collaboration and better bottom-line results.

Ride on the Open Road—
The Discovery Mindset

It is rare that people are willing to ride the self-discovery motorcycle; it is too scary and unpredictable. You have to be somewhat of a rebel to get on a motorcycle to begin with, and there aren't too many rebels around the office.

The person on the self-discovery motorcycle is an innovator. He doesn't travel by car anymore. He only owns a "bike." Something has come over him; he has a different mindset. In fact, you might find him a bit too aggressive for your taste. He can challenge your way of thinking, and from there change the traditional corporate mindset altogether. The guy evokes personal growth and group innovation in everyone he meets. His motorcycle takes you down the untraveled road, winding and swerving. It's the place where the pavement ends and the rough road begins. To get there you have to turn away from the usual course, make a major change in direction and deviate from convention. The road to discovery may not be on the map.

Just sitting on the seat and holding the handle bars makes a person feel more daring and eager to ride. The best place to go is out on the wide-open country roads where you can really let loose, not be afraid to step on the gas and bend your bike with every turn— horizontal to the ground. Be a rebel.

Getting on this road is up to you. You're a lot freer on the bike, which is good because we're talking about a mindset change. So get rid of all your baggage, both physical and emotional; it will just get in the way during this trip. You have to clear your head, start with a fresh and open mind, and think differently. Try to view discovery and innovation not as a process or business activity, but as a way of thinking. A discovery mindset sets you apart from others on the paved road, and speeds you ahead of competition.

Be Free to Innovate

What is innovation? Dictionaries describe it is as a new idea, method or device. We believe it is all about creating and capturing new value for your customers. But it is also a mindset, a pervasive attitude and way of thinking focused beyond the present and into the future. Though you can't touch it, smell it, hear it or taste it, you can sense, think and feel innovation. The part of innovation that frightens most CEOs is its unavoidable association with risk. Motorcycles are a risky way to travel; cars are safer and more comfortable. Many CEOs in large corporations ride in cars. They pay lip service to the power of innovation, but are averse to the type of aggressive investment it demands. Instead, they dabble in innovation. They stay safely on the highway, throwing occasional resources and dollars into innovation, but their commitment usually ends there. It's one thing to talk about innovation, but it's quite another to stake your resources—and your career—on it. This requires becoming a committed and long-term innovator.

The reason innovation is consistently misunderstood is that for years managers have been looking from the wrong vantage point. They have been in their cars! Every year they take out the latest thing from their trunk: new techniques or processes, new organization structures, new research approaches and new jargon that explains how each of these will stimulate innovation. But none of these tangible solutions will fix the real problem, usually because they never last longer than a few months. Solutions can't be found in the trunk of the car. A motorcycle has no room for this "baggage," and that's why a biker is free to develop the mindset that sustains discovery and innovation. Remember, innovation is intangible. Intuitive. A state of mind. A pervasive, forward-thinking attitude. You will only find it on the open road, so get out there now. Try being a biker for a while. You might discover that you prefer to travel this way! It is a lot of fun, too, especially when you let loose and step on the gas.

F = FREE. Use your whole brain to forge courageously ahead and draw your team members together. Ride on the open road of discovery. Use creativity and be free.

CHAPTER 6
"T" FOR TRUST

"Leadership is much more an art, a belief, a condition of the heart than a set of things to do. The visible signs of artful leadership are expressed, ultimately, in its practice."

Max De Pree, author of *Leadership Is An Art*

Sonny Garg, former Chief Innovation and Information Officer at Exelon and current Energy Solutions Head at Uptake underscored: "Once an organization has developed a culture in which a majority of the people do not feel the drive of common values and goals, it can be quite difficult to change their sentiment and mindset." In this situation a disingenuous culture exists, and a lack of trust prevails. Sonny believes that employees are smart and tuned-in to an organization's culture. We think so too, and have observed many times that once actions or norms go against established values, trust is broken.

Leaders need to cultivate trust. This takes not only time, but a concerted effort from leaders to match behaviors and intended values. Trust starts with building a relationship that has mutual benefit—not one-way gain.

How Leaders Build Trust

In order to provide trust and respect to others, leaders need to be fair, open and honest with people. If there are major changes coming internally, it is best not to surprise employees, but rather engage them in conversation. By being part of the discussion, trust and respect are fostered. "Talk openly and honesty among each other, and confront people in meetings," shared Kristi Lafleur, former head of the Illinois Tollway. She adds, "My approach is to be fair and honest with people. You won't always be able to tell people what they want to hear or do what they want to do, but you can try and explain the process and create an atmosphere where they will be dealt with fairly. We use the screen of 'what our customers would want.'"

Communication is particularly important when it comes to trust. Linda Mallers, CEO of FarmLogix, told us that she avoids any negative talk about other colleagues when they are not around. "Don't talk about any co-workers in a way you wouldn't want to be talked about." How do you communicate in a catastrophe? "Be open and honest. Get everything out all at once. Don't share a little information today and a little more tomorrow, because the messages tend to snowball."

Jen Bentz of Tyson Foods uses a different method of communication. "We work across multiple locations. We're not face-to-face, so we use technology (e.g. video conferencing or blogs) to reach out to others and collaborate. Ideas come from everywhere. We've got to feel confident that every single person in the organization has a voice. We have regular meetings where people share what's new in the market domestically and globally, and how that can spark ideas. We are always looking for avenues from where we can build and engage with each other." Collaboration, she contends, creates a sense of trust.

Another component of trust is transparency — letting those you work with know what is going on and providing the openness to communicate problems and issues in a safe way. One CEO has office hours several times a week where anyone can come and speak about any topic. Kristi Lafleur had set up different channels that allow employees to report misconduct and raise issues at the Illinois Tollway when necessary.

Trust can also mean giving employees and colleagues alike the space to do their job by using a hands-off approach. We call this, "disciplined freedom." According to Pete Kadens, CEO of Green Thumb Industries, this is accomplished by creating a "yes culture," not a "no culture." He elaborates, "don't micromanage. Create a mutual relationship of reciprocity and trust, and use empathy. As an entrepreneur you are forced into an extreme state of self-awareness. Ultimately, everyone cares about himself or herself. While you can't make everyone's priorities number one, you can be a good listener. You can build up confidence when people know their organization cares about them. Ask the right questions about them and their family."

We applaud this group of thoughtful leaders. They are transparent, empathetic, open, honest, positive, communicative, collaborative and transparent. At other organizations, however, a "lack of trust" often exists and has a negative impact on the culture.

Lack of Trust

Employees are frustrated when they feel management doesn't trust them, as they should! Employees perceive that they are not given enough responsibility. They are told to do monotonous tasks and quickly tire of them. When a mid-level project manager was asked what would give her an increased sense of purpose in her job, she said: "I'd like more responsibilities and a higher level of trust by management to let me make my own decisions. Right now we are treated more like children than intelligent, quick-thinking employees. If I could be given added responsibility and autonomy, I would enjoy this job a lot more." Other interviewees frequently expressed this sentiment.

Employees at organizations with clear sets of norms and values most often worked harder, even when management was not supervising them. The magnetic values in their workplace served as a source of motivation. These values or beliefs fostered greater togetherness and connection. In contrast, at companies with few to zero well-established norms or values, employees tended to "goof off" whenever they had the chance to do so. Employees who feel and believe that their bosses trust them are far more motivated to perform at peak efficiency.

Anomie—A State of Normlessness

Trust and togetherness cannot happen if anomie exists. Anomie means alienation or normlessness. It results when individuals and groups don't have a belief system (values) and behavior guidelines (norms). Anomie leaves individuals feeling distant, disillusioned and disjointed. It leaves organizations dysfunctional, distracted and disrupted. It stems from groups and individuals that lack cohesive social and interpersonal guidelines for interaction. Without a solid foundation of values or beliefs, meaningful norms cannot be developed. Anomie emerges and runs rampant without an integrated set of norms to guide interpersonal communication and behaviors.

When anomie creeps into an organization, it weakens the ties and social bonds that usually hold workers together and keep them going. If people do not feel compelled to conform to established norms, social cohesion and organizational integrity break down. Neither trust nor togetherness can form. Anomie appears when individuals are not in some way connected as a group. Ironically, a lack of group cohesion also impedes the empowerment of individuals, and halts the development of personal identities, missions or purposes. Norms and values provide "bonding power" for members of a group, and this empowers both the team and the individual. When anomie dilutes and waters down the social glue, trust falls apart.

Individuals, organizations and society as a whole urgently need to become aware of the threatening persistence of anomie. It is a complicated dilemma that deserves attention and individual priority. To a great extent, however, it remains a hidden and infrequently discussed social disease. Anomie stands virtually free and clear of public awareness. Most organizations don't even recognize that anomie pervades their corridor walls, prevails throughout team meetings and preoccupies the minds and spirits of employees. And if they do catch a glimmer of the symptoms of anomie, it is brushed under the rug and ignored.

We need both values and norms to instill a sense of trust in the workplace.

Employees on an Island

Isolation runs parallel with anomie. Without norms, people believe that they live and work on an island—totally disconnected psychologically and emotionally from the group, despite being a part of one physically. In order to overcome anomie, one must become a member and feel part of a group or team. The challenge is determining how best to relate to and interact with other members of the group. In turn, this requires that each member of an organization learns how to interact effectively with others. Identifying how best to "fit in" with a group is hard, but it's important to strive for integration rather than isolation.

Over time, group members will hopefully develop a sense of community. This "community" can be defined as a group of individuals who share common goals, experiences, mission, vision, likes, dislikes and most importantly values. But without a shared set of norms and values, feelings of isolation are perpetuated as anomie continues. When groups forego developing a set of agreed-upon values and norms, behavior and communication becomes random, inconsistent and arbitrary. Employees never know from one day to the next how they will be treated by managers and vice-versa. Signals are mixed, communications are misinterpreted and behavior becomes erratic. People tend to become more and more isolated from each other.

The Individual's Impact

Every individual within the work place can shape, form and influence the organization. The best way to demonstrate this influence is not by trying to figure out the contributions or "value" of each individual to the whole, but rather by realizing the negative impact on the organization of an individual not participating as an active member of a particular group.

Let's try this example: it might seem trite to talk about the value of a receptionist in a firm of nationally recognized professionals, but take away the receptionist and watch those professionals attempt to answer the phone, field questions, convey a consistent image and respond effectively to client questions. Trying to calibrate and measure the impact of the absence of an individual within the organization is a good way to identify the impact and value of that person within the group.

Amazingly, while most employees and managers we interviewed felt that a desire for well-defined norms and values was an important factor when deciding to join an organization, few people ever asked about or explored their own company's norms or values during the interview process. We found that people are reluctant to ask employers about such "touchy-feely" issues as norms and values.

You can't imagine the number of times we asked people about their personal and professional values, only to receive a blank stare and a response of "I've never been asked that question before."

Without organizational norms and values, individuals are forced to create their own. In other words, norms and values look like a clear summer sky, late at night. The individual stars are distinct and bright, but none are connected to each other. If they were in some way, their brightness would enlighten the sky, creating a distinct and precise constellation. While each individual does have a desired set of personal values, there is no inherent glue or linkage of one individual's norms to another, nor to an entire group. When organizations do provide strong collective norms and values that bring individuals out of isolation, effective collaboration shines true.

If done correctly, this kind of power can really be felt. You can sense it very clearly in organizations that have it. Employees have a unique sense of loyalty and dedication to the organization; they trust each other and actually enjoy their work. It becomes a meaningful part of their daily lives because it offers self-actualization potential. It satisfies their need for belonging to a group in a meaningful way, which turns apathetic employees into highly motivated ones.

Togetherness — The Power of Shared Leadership

Contrary to popular belief, being a leader does not mean you are at the top looking down. You don't exercise control over those who work with you, nor do you wield power over them. Fear is a tool that motivates an individual to do just enough to avoid consequences. Shared success, on the other hand, is a goal everyone will strive for. "Unfortunately, I think the world is full of people that care more about themselves than about the company or the people within the company," one CEO contends. "It is important for me to make high-level decisions, but the company can't succeed unless everyone is doing a great job as well. People will find me running the photocopier at night or when I am getting ready for a board meeting. We recycle around here and people catch me carrying my recycling bin and dumping it out like everybody else. They seem to feel that that's odd, but it's not. Why should I ask somebody else to do it?"

Hierarchies put up walls between members of a team. They stifle the exchange of ideas and the collective power of teams. The limiting aspect of this rigid structure is not lost on workers. When employees know that there is no system in place for their voices to be heard, what confidence will they have that a leader has all the information necessary to make the best decision? "The moment you take a hierarchical approach, you have created a problem," Dipak Jain, former Director of Sasin at Chulalongkorn University explains. "People are not sure whether you are saying what you believe, or saying what you are supposed to because of your position. So, people get confused. Is the message you are sending the real message or the one you think should be delivered?"

He stressed: "If you explain the decision-making process that you went through, then when people see the result they will buy into it because they know this is how it happened. The process has to be transparent. There is a way for people to contribute, to say, 'my ideas and thoughts all went into the decision, my inputs got included, and the output was something that I was a part of.'"

When inclusiveness and trust exist within an organization, individuals feel attached and connected. They know that they belong and play an important role in the growth of their organization. They are involved in shaping the culture in which they work.

Many times, culture means one thing to senior management and something very different to employees. Inclusiveness enables people to have a voice and trust gives that voice weight and confidence. At work, employees should feel that a decision was not a one-person pronouncement. There must be opportunities for group members to listen to others and contribute. This further builds trust. People need to know that their comments are heard and their contributions are valued. When making a decision, leaders should be able to say: "I listened to everyone. This is what I heard, this is what I am doing and this is why I am doing it." We call this shared leadership.

Trust and togetherness exist to nurture *both* the individual and the group. This inclusiveness happens when deep, selfless listening takes place. But here's the key: leaders must acknowledge and act upon the needs of others and communicate the value of their perspectives, thoughts and opinions. This action step is crucial to creating real trust and not just feeble talk. The takeaway is, leaders must be open and respectful of differences and view others as a valuable part of the team. Under this scenario, a sense of trust prevails in the culture.

T = TRUST. Trust is the primary thread in the fabric of a culture. Success is a byproduct of everyone doing his or her part. The individual's impact is honored, trust is built and leadership is shared.

CHAPTER 7
"U" FOR USE REWARDS

"If the frontline people do count, you couldn't prove it by examining the reward systems in most organizations."

Karl Albrecht, German entrepreneur and founder of ALDI discount supermarket chain

Rewards and recognition are the essential ingredients to fuel a collaborative, praised-based culture. We detail a how-to-praise guide in the next chapter that discusses seven ways to praise more effectively. But why reward employees in the first place? For now, let's look at rewards, both financial and non-financial, by asking the question: How do rewards motivate, recognize and shape individuals within their work cultures? Linda Mallers is the Founder and CEO of FarmLogix, a Chicago-based start-up that is a one-stop shopping platform that connects restaurants and schools to an online network of more than 300 small local farms. According to her, "people respond to praise and love to hear it. Recognition isn't just verbal, it's giving people responsibilities." In addition to praise, we believe specific tangible rewards are essential for building an effective culture.

Sonny Garg, Energy Solutions Head at Uptake, confirms the indispensable role of tangible rewards: "Praise is necessary, but not sufficient. People still want to make more money and move up in their career. If all they get is praise, it can be demotivating overtime." For example, Uptake makes and gives out 3-D printed trophies for certain accomplishments, and winners get time with members of the executive committee to talk about their ideas. Each employee is recognized and valued as a result.

Selectivity and Scarcity of Rewards

Sometimes simply spending time with employees can be a form of reward. Shares Sam Yagan, co-founder of OKCupid and current CEO of Shoprunner.com, "In theory, I can hand out praise all the time. But not everyone can get on my calendar, not everybody gets that opportunity." To combat this, he does a "Lunch With Sam" every month. He recognizes and rewards the successful efforts of his employees by offering up his valuable free time to engage with them on a personal level. When Sam was growing up he won many selective awards, and he acknowledges that this recognition positively impacted his identity. "You're the valedictorian, you won the spelling bee, you won the math contest, you won this and that…if there was an award to win growing up, I won it." These "contests," while competitive and selective, were "always very legitimate, real and authentic." These instances of recognition and praise directly impacted his bottom line–his identity!

Giving Recognition through Rewards

Here's the crux of our research findings with respect to rewards: management needs to put some money where its mouth is. Rewards need to be significant enough to provide substantive and adequate recognition and motivation. The key is that senior management must endorse and regularly use these rewards. They must be visible. Specifically, rewards can be both financial, such as bonuses and incentives, and non-financial, such as extra vacations or other gifts, as categorized here:

FINANCIAL-BASED REWARDS:
- Stock ownership options
- Performance-based bonuses
- Long-term financial bonuses
- Cash awards for outstanding work
- Team performance-based bonuses

NON-FINANCIAL BASED REWARDS:

- Letters or emails that praise an accomplishment
- Group trips and travel awards
- Extra vacation days
- Peer recognition lunches
- Senior management dinners
- Increased training and development
- Special peer recognition plaques, honors and awards
- Increased job responsibilities
- Greater budgetary control
- Group social events

Effective Recognition Programs

Let's take a close look at the recognition programs and rewards that we have seen work over the years. Management often uses them to inspire employees to embrace innovation. The following are examples within four types of rewards and recognition programs that can be executed in an innovation culture, focusing on individual recognition, peer recognition, professional development and family programs.

1. *Individual recognition*—vacation days, special gifts, trips and travel, managing future projects and gaining more responsibility in innovation

2. *Peer recognition*—announcement of achievements in company newsletter and bulletins, dinner or lunch with senior leadership, public praise among co-workers

3. *Professional development*—additional training in innovation including the opportunity to visit benchmark organizations

4. *Family programs*—invitations to events with family (such as a soccer game), scholarships for one's kids, participation in summer programs to work on a project at the company, internships for one's kids

In addition to these programs, celebratory innovation events tied to successful new product or service launches offer opportunities for recognizing teams and people. Companies can hold an all-firm innovation awards ceremony or similar event to recognize innovation efforts, or arrange more intimate special dinners with senior management and team members to acknowledge their successful efforts.

The Impact of Rewards

Huge internal personal benefits accrue from setting up a reward structure. Some example benefits include:

- Increased pride
- Peer recognition
- Higher self-confidence and self-worth
- More motivation to perform
- Heightened awareness of desired norms
- Greater job satisfaction
- Enhanced self-accomplishment

Team leaders need to give far more thought into effective ways of giving meaningful recognition. Rewards, both monetary and non-monetary, are powerful tools to energize team members.

Recognition and the Larger Picture

Recognition does wonders to build self-confidence and self-esteem. When we recognize others, it can impact an individual's self-worth on a profound level. We describe it as *feedback that sinks to the core*.

The purpose of recognition should be to accentuate tasks completed, recommendations given, gestures made or goals achieved. In order to provide maximum benefit, recognition needs to be genuine, objective and visible. This, in turn, leads to higher self-worth. Greater self-worth contributes to greater confidence in and satisfaction with one's contributions.

Recognition can be offered in a variety of ways and under differing circumstances. It can also occur throughout the different stages of a task or project. In fact, providing recognition to employees along the way is often far more motivating than waiting until after the task has been finished. There are three milestones throughout the innovation process where opportunities for recognition can exist: upon recognizing insights for *identifying* a problem, after understanding and overcoming difficulties encountered *during* creative solution generation and when recognizing and activating the benefits accrued from pinpointing *solutions* to the problem.

Hunt for and seek ways to recognize others. It bolsters and strengthens team members. They feel better about themselves and in turn, perform more effectively and efficiently. When team members are filled with self-doubt and question themselves, they under-perform. Their concentration becomes fragmented. Time and energy are also often spent wondering if their actions will ever be recognized, positively or not. To avoid these draining, unnecessary situations, serve up lots of recognition.

Leaders need recognition too. Does this sound surprising? Hopefully not. Most people expect the flow of recognition to stem from the top down. How often do you complement your boss for a job well done? If it is infrequent, know that recognition motivates bosses too. Frequent recognition leaves groups stronger, more confident and better motivated to perform. The key is to view recognition as a powerful, high-octane fuel.

How Rewards Fuel Innovation

Achieving success in innovation takes a lot of hard work, time, resources and effort. Although many team members can feel accomplished by working on a new idea, this is often not enough to warrant the amount of work that goes into it. We took a special look at rewards as they relate to innovation, and learned that they come in many different varieties and structures. For some companies, financial rewards have proven to spur innovative energy and encourage a culture of innovation. Other companies, however, found that psychic rewards, such as praise and time off, yield far better results than financial rewards.

To drive innovation, more and more companies are looking to grow organically from within their own organization. Although mergers, acquisitions and partnerships have the ability to provide incremental revenues to an organization, most innovation comes from within—from the organizations' own employees.

Because employees are so critical in driving innovation, they need to be encouraged and motivated to do so. Without motivation, employees can become disengaged and lack passion. They may work to get the job done, but not go above-and-beyond to innovate and take risks.

Motivation is essential in convincing employees to actively engage in innovation initiatives like idea generation and new product launches, especially if it is one that requires risk and experimentation. Without the proper culture in place, innovation initiatives are less likely to happen or succeed.

Create an Entrepreneurial Environment

Establishing rewards and incentives based on performance is key to increasing team member motivation and promoting a positive innovation culture. Entrepreneurs often take risks and put forth effort in hopes of receiving a profitable return—this same type of environment can be replicated within a large organization by rewarding employees with equity.

There are many ways in which employees serving on an innovation team can be rewarded for their successful efforts, both individually and as a group. One option for individuals is to receive an annual variable bonus paid out over five years based on an actual percentage of profits generated from new products and services launched into the marketplace.

Another effective way to deliver innovation rewards is to give them to the entire team. This would include a reward based on actual sales or profits achieved from the entire portfolio of innovations created. For example, if $20 million in profits is generated and 2%, or $400,000, are distributed to the innovation team, then each of the ten members would receive a $40,000 bonus. The key here is that financial rewards are directly tied to the success of the innovation portfolio that is developed by the team. If it performs well, they get a large bonus. If it fails, they do not. It's as simple as that!

Lastly, there are programs that are geared towards having employees feel more of a sense of "ownership" of their innovations. This includes things like innovation phantom stock that gives employees an option to invest in "owning" or securing a portion of future innovation profits to build internal commitment. This greater investment from employees (both literally and figuratively) is a terrific way to get them engaged in the innovation process and have them root for project successes, along with their senior management.

Avoid Five Mistakes Often Made With Innovation-Related Rewards

Many companies with world-class innovation cultures have specific reward programs to nurture innovation. Other companies, however, are slow to activate reward programs to incentivize innovation. Without a formal plan for rewarding and recognizing innovation, it can be difficult to incorporate an innovation mindset into the culture. While organizations often provide some types of rewards, many of these are ineffective or do not promote innovation specifically or effectively. If rewards don't align with the organization's goals, further support a team-oriented mindset or acknowledge performance in the market place, then they are the *wrong* rewards. Five examples of rewards that companies should *avoid* include:

1. *Rewarding individual ideas* — instead, <u>reward the success of commercialized new products and services launched in the market</u>. Many companies provide financial incentives for the initial idea. Although at first glance this sounds good, organizations should be rewarding a team's development of an idea, not the individual who originally came up with it. Any idea will undergo many changes on the road to commercialization. Often, the original idea won't even be recognizable by the time it gets to the marketplace. Simply put, reward the result, not the idea.

2. *Rewarding people solely on overall company performance* — instead, <u>reward specific innovation results relative to the original goals set</u>. Rewards for overall company performance will not necessarily incentivize employees to pursue innovation. As a general rule, the goals and objectives of the organization must tie into the types of rewards that are given. For example, if seeking to spur a culture of innovation, there must be financial rewards in place that help define how individuals and teams contribute to the overall growth and development of the company's innovation culture specifically.

3. *Providing a bonus that has a small percentage allocated to innovation* — instead, <u>increase the variable bonus portion coming from innovation to between fifty and one hundred percent</u>. Although variable bonuses are great tools to motivate employees, they are often not tied directly to innovation. In order for a variable bonus to foster a culture of innovation, there should be some element of the bonus tied directly to tangible innovation outputs as well as performance metrics. Linking ten percent of the bonus to innovation is not enough. If a bonus only has a small percentage allocated toward innovation, this signals that innovation is not important. The proportional impact of innovation should reflect the priority of innovation in the organization.

4. *Ignoring team-based rewards* — instead, <u>use team-based rewards to reflect actual market performance.</u> Cross-functional teams are

the kindling of the innovation culture fire. They are needed to launch successful innovations and must be empowered with the proper resources. In order to further ignite a culture of innovation that includes teamwork and collaboration, use team-based rewards as a motivating tool to further ensure that employees work together.

5. *Giving rewards that aren't specifically tied to an innovation portfolio*—instead, <u>reward the results of an innovation portfolio based on real-world performance</u>. Many companies make the mistake of giving rewards for any type of new product or service rather than differentiating between incremental and disruptive. Innovations that are disruptive are more difficult to create, so they should be rewarded at a higher level than incremental innovations when successful. It is important to strategically define a mission and vision for innovation and reward successes accordingly. For example, if all new products are given the same reward, it may create a mindset and culture in which employees create incremental lower-risk new products and line extensions, thereby avoiding the more difficult but higher return-generating disruptive innovations.

U = USE REWARDS. Be mindful of the powerful impact of rewards and put a creative, motivational reward and recognition plan in place. Learn how rewards specifically nurture innovation and avoid the five mistakes often made with innovation-related rewards.

CHAPTER 8
"P" FOR PRAISE

"Unless a reviewer has the courage to give you unqualified praise, I say ignore the bastard."

**John Steinbeck, author and
Nobel Prize in Literature recipient**

Margaret Heater has been a leader in the field of human resources for over forty years, and a nonprofit volunteer for close to thirty. This sage-extraordinaire on the topic of praise believes: "A lot of people are uncomfortable with praise, or they do not know how to praise, or they've never received enough praise themselves to recognize the opportunity to give it."

To understand the nuances of praise, we interviewed a select group of leaders in varying fields through which we uncovered seven ways to give praise more effectively. We learned that praise is what human beings need to feel worthwhile. It is a source of energy, a vital "food for the psyche." Authentic praise has the power to build employee self-confidence, convey genuine personal interest in team members and demonstrate that you care about them. The best part is, praising doesn't require a monumental effort. You can achieve all of this simply by sending a note, giving a call or asking how you can help. You get the picture—small gestures combine to yield big results! *Who Moved My Cheese* author, Ken Blanchard, dishes up a helpful summary of praise: "Feedback is the breakfast of champions."

Most of the leaders that we interviewed recognized the value of praise, yet simultaneously said they needed to provide it more often. They acknowledged that they were not providing *enough* praise to their colleagues and peers.

Inspired by our interviews, we created a how-to-praise guide that combines some of the praising best practices leaders are using today, as well as some useful techniques they were hoping to adopt in the near future:

1. Plan to be spontaneous and timely when giving praise.

2. Be public—praise in front of others.

3. Balance positive and constructive feedback, but start with positive praise.

4. Keep it up—praise consistently.

5. Focus on achievements and accomplishments.

6. Use descriptive—not global—praise to motivate and facilitate personal growth.

7. Deliver authentic praise based on behavior.

These seven initiatives can serve as a checklist for praising effectively.

1. Plan to be spontaneous and timely when giving praise.

"Say it on the spot! Plan for spontaneity," remarks cultural anthropologist, Mary Catherine Bateson. "Instead of coming out of a conversation with someone and making a mental note to send them a memo and tell them they're doing a good job, go in prepared to say it on the spot." Let people know how they're doing, and let them know frequently. Spontaneity often creates a feeling of sincerity, even intimacy, in the process of giving praise. The "giver" has reached out and shared some personal information, and was willing to be open, transparent and vulnerable.

As a rule, praise should be immediate and based on a task that a person has recently done. The mantra is, catch a team member doing the right or positive thing, and acknowledge it. It is best if the "giver" can share it in the context of when it happens or relatively soon afterwards. Margaret Heater, retired human resource manager, shared: "When someone says to me, 'Margi, I've noticed something about you and it impressed me; I want to know more about it' Wow! My whole being gets excited over that." She calls this "accidental praise" or praise that involves surprise, quiet achievement or catching people doing something right when they least expect it. It happens when we take time to actively observe and focus on other people or team members.

"Be attentive and observant, but also debrief in a timely manner," stresses former two-time space shuttle and international space station astronaut Mary Ellen Weber. She stressed that a sense of urgency should drive praise, noting the importance of "debriefing" the situation. This sense of urgency, getting the praise delivered as soon as possible, is vital—particularly in a serious, potentially dangerous situation. Debrief quickly and move forward. The timing of praise, particularly when in situations that require immediate application of that praise, is essential.

2. Be public—praise in front of others.

In most cases, a senior leader will privately call an employee into their office for an annual evaluation. As Mary Catherine Bateson wonders, "You've got multiple desks in an open space, so why not walk down the aisle and say in a loud clear voice, 'Hey Bill, that report you just sent me hit the nail on the head!' It doesn't have to be ceremonially public. Two senior people in the company can be talking in the elevator and they can say something about Bill's work; it'll get to him."

What is the impact of public praise? People see that the workplace culture is one that rewards and recognizes effort and accomplishment. There is also an increasing sense that recognition is paramount to nurturing commitment. However, there is a need to be told the truth—to not be left confused—as to what is expected and rewarded. Public praise also creates a ripple effect. The more people see and hear others giving and receiving praise, the more they will come to expect it as a norm and be comfortable giving praise themselves. This is how you nurture a culture of praise and recognition.

The Chicago Innovation Awards is an outstanding example of the power of public praise. Each year, twenty organizations are selected to receive this highly prestigious award out of over five hundred nominees across all industries. The award conveys that their product, service or business not only solves a customer or consumer problem or need, but is a unique offering in the marketplace and has had a significant financial impact. It brings together large and small companies, whether they are high-tech, low-tech or no-tech to celebrate their breakthrough innovation.

These companies' efforts are recognized in front of 1500 people in the stunning Harris Theater in Chicago, their achievements are promoted to the media, and they also get to ring the closing NASDAQ bell in New York City. When you expose people to that level of public recognition for their innovation efforts, you can see how it affects their team and company. Innovation award winners frequently describe how the award has helped motivate their employees, attract new talent, encourage new investors, reinforce customer relationships and bolster a positive culture. These awards confirm the powerful impact of public recognition.

3. Balance positive and constructive feedback, but start with positive praise.

Positive praise hits the mark, but be constructive as well. Here is Bateson's approach: "As a teacher, when people hand in papers you go through them and you mark things that are wrong. I decided after a couple years in college teaching, I can't help marking the stuff that's wrong because I'm always correcting my own writing. But then I would say, 'Ok Bateson, go back over this paper and find some things that make you want to write "Yes!" in the margins. And make darn sure that when you make your comments at the end, it has a positive element as well as a negative. Think back to your own school experience—there were all those little negatives undermining you.'" The takeaway sounds rather simple, and it is: too often, we forget the positive affirmations. Have a balance of positive and constructive comments.

4. Keep it up—praise consistently.

If praise is given once or twice, it's not going to do much to change the person or the culture. But once it begins to feel like a continuing pattern, you are going to get a higher level of confidence and morale. It brews a sense of excitement about both the future and what's been done, as well as a sense of forward movement where other people will follow. Mary Catherine Bateson elaborates on her previous example, "Sally is the next desk over from Bill, and she's likely to turn over to him and say 'the boss is right, that was a good report,' which she otherwise might not do." When we create this pattern, there exists an *expectation* that the high quality (of the work) is going to continue. We have also gotten the team involved in praising, which is a powerful tool as well for developing a widespread culture of praise and recognition. The takeaway is: create a pattern with giving praise. Be consistent, and keep it up. It is good for personal growth, team morale and future product quality. Just think, all this from a few words of acknowledgement.

Is there a downside to praise? Portraiture artist and elementary school teacher Barbara Slater had this to share: "The downside is that you wonder if you can continue to perform on this level, or if this is a one shot deal. You put the pressure on yourself to continue to strive to the level that someone has acknowledged, yet you wonder if you can do it again or if you can excel to get more praise."

As a painter, Barbara takes quite a few classes and each time is constantly reaching for excellence. "You want to hear that praise again, and you want to hear it on this other level. So the uncertainty is certainly there, and I think that's the other side of praise." Along with the praise comes the drive to want to have it happen again, consciously or intuitively. Artists, as far as praise is concerned, accept this uncertainty as a natural part of the creative process. She notes: "It's kind of an interpersonal feeling—I don't think anyone in a creative mode ever feels that they have arrived. So you're constantly working on things and you want the praise as you go along because that's what fuels it." Barbara isn't looking for praise to tell her that she has "arrived" or accomplished something of worth. Instead, she uses praise not only as a source of validation but as a driver to continue to perform better and better. The same should be true of employees and team members. The crucial message for team members is: keep praise up and be consistent.

5. Focus on achievements and accomplishments.

Unlike spontaneous praise, the annual performance review should focus in great detail on people's achievements, accomplishments, strengths and assets—all the things they did well over the course of the year. Too often though, the emphasis of a performance review is put on what needs to be corrected or improved. Shared one executive, "Time and again in the annual performance review, there are three positives and three weaknesses. A person leaves that review totally ignoring the positives, but rather focused only on those three weakness areas." For that reason, achievements and strengths should be emphasized in an annual performance review while constructive feedback should be given in real time when the behavior or action occurs. Don't wait.

Annual reviews are a powerful tool to help people experience and achieve personal success. When people feel good about themselves because of a success in the workplace, this positivity will spill over into other areas. These individuals will start to perform better, seek out more responsibility and accomplish more in their workplace. As a result of continued successes, they are more apt to take risks. They will try to do things that are more difficult because of the confidence they have developed from earlier success. Risk taking results in learning. If adults would take more risks, there would be greater learning on a regular basis.

By identifying employees' greatest strengths and assigning them responsibilities and tasks that leverage those strengths, leaders will increase the chances of their team members' success. It is important to monitor, even "engineer" or arrange small successes to some extent. It does no good to put employees into situations, roles, groups or activities where there is a good chance of failure. Continuous failure breeds only one thing—a lack of self-confidence. This, in turn, leads to more failures. It becomes a self-fulfilling prophecy; as self-confidence is weakened, it becomes more and more difficult for the individual to achieve success.

Managing and "staging" a few small wins for employees increases their internal value and self-worth. This improves their self-esteem and fortifies their own skill base, which begins to feed positively on itself, bringing more successes to individuals.

Annual reviews are a great opportunity to provide praise. They help employees acknowledge their accomplishments and achievements. Over time, employees inculcate this successfulness and positivity into their ongoing behavior. Success becomes expected by the individuals themselves and tends to be self-perpetuated.

6. Use descriptive—not global—praise to motivate and facilitate personal growth.

A leader can facilitate the development of his or her team members success "perpetuation" by using descriptive praise. If a person has done something well, rather than giving just global praise (e.g. "you did a great job") it is much better to describe what you saw and felt when it happened. Describing the work in detail adds a whole new dimension to the person's view of him or herself. It creates a more motivated individual, and it allows for greater learning to occur.

If a person gives a presentation on a difficult topic to a large group, one response might be, "Good work!" This is global praise. It is not a bad response, but it *limits* learning and growth from the inside. Specific, descriptive praise would be much better because the person would learn more about herself. Accordingly, the leader could respond by saying something like: "You presented some difficult material in an organized way, we learned a lot, enjoyed ourselves and felt hopeful. Your style of speaking was warm and engaging, and you fostered interaction among the group participants." The person's view of herself has added a new dimension—she is becoming a skillful, effective presenter. Now, she knows exactly what she did well and is motivated to further fine-tune her presenting skills.

Detailed or descriptive praise leads to more personal learning and greater motivation than global praise. Summarizes artist and teacher, Barbara Slater: "Praise for specific things, like 'the students were very attentive,' or 'they got their work done quickly,' or 'they used color boldly and creatively'—these details are motivating to kids."

But why is this detail or description so important when giving praise? Specificity is what substantiates the sincerity and authenticity. Consider more generic praise, like: "Oh, he's wonderful, he's great", or "you're amazing, you're unbelievable." One might ask: "Well, how do you know?" or "Why?" Instead, try: "You know, you were great because of the way you put those spotlights on the speakers last night during the annual meeting. You were able to really bring them to life. The presenters looked awesome, plus it helped us focus on their content and message because we could really see and hear each of them." Not only does this specify things an individual did well, but it shows an active effort from the "praiser." He was clearly engaged and those detailed, thoughtful comments display to the individual that his boss cares about his work and continued improvement, thus building mutual trust and improving their overall relationship.

7. Deliver authentic praise based on behavior.

Never praise just for the sake of praising, and always use the language that "fits" or has meaning to the recipient. Barbara Slater shares the praise guidelines she used when teaching grades one through nine and serving as a school counselor: "There were many different situations in the classroom and as a counselor. I *never* praised for anything that didn't have a value. When I praised I didn't put it into formal words, I tried to use the student's jargon. For example, I would say, 'this is really cool! I'm really enjoying this; you did great!' using their vernacular, their language."

It's best to critique the behavior, not the person. Praise can come in many shapes or sizes, indirectly or upfront. "So when there was a discipline situation or when I was dealing with negative behavior, I could still stress, 'I really like you and I like what you did the other day' or something of that nature, so there was always a positive with the negative." Praise should focus on the behavior, not the character of any one person.

Nurture a sense of trust and sincerity. Don't water down praise, stressed Slater: "People intuitively know when someone's being sincere. Kids especially know it. And don't keep saying the same thing over and over again. Say it differently, use illustrative words and descriptive action steps, and more self-knowledge will occur."

P = PRAISE. Taken together, our seven tools for praising help cultivate self-knowledge so a person can grow and learn. Try being spontaneous, descriptive and consistent with your praise, and remember to do so authentically and contextually.

CHAPTER 9
THE POWER OF PRAISE

"When virtues are pointed out first, flaws seem less insurmountable."

**Judith Martin (pen name, Miss Manners),
journalist, author and etiquette authority**

Giving and receiving praise has the power to motivate the person, energize the team and nurture a collaborative culture. Now that's a triple "wow" in any playbook! Recognition in the workplace needs to become commonplace rather than a rarity. Give it as often as you can. Find new ways to provide people with positive feedback and an uplifting experience. It can be verbal, such as, "Way to go." "Here's how you made an impact," "I'm impressed with the presentation that you made yesterday," or "I think that is a big improvement." It can be conveyed facially or physically. Shake someone's hand. Give them a hug. Offer a genuine smile signaling a job well done. Give them a pat on the back. All forms of proactive praise can boost the strengths of one another and positively contribute to overall performance.

Using Praise to Generate Motivation, Create Energy and Innovate the Culture

Motivationally, praise changes a person's self-perception. Praise helps us identify the things we are good at and helps us understand how certain qualities have developed into personal strengths. Or, as Deepak Chopra so succinctly and emphatically stressed in the foreword to our book, *Apples Are Square: Thinking Differently About Leadership*: "Great leaders are self-aware." Importantly, the awareness or consciousness of our unique gifts further motivates us to develop them. Orla Branigan, head of public relations for Mexico's business school EGADE at the Technologico de Monterrey, emphasizes, "praise has such a powerful emotional impact and creates psychological change in terms of how we see ourselves. It becomes an intrinsic source of motivation. Praise becomes the set of standards the organization is setting for me, and these standards go beyond compensation or loyalty benefits." Praise, then, serves as motivational fiber for each individual within an organization. It becomes a compelling inner driver for personal growth and learning. When praise is in place, the individual becomes fired-up.

Besides motivating and energizing at our personal core, praise also creates positive and electrifying energy to fire-up the team. This is to say that praise allows enthusiasm and optimism to permeate. Observes Jeff Semenchuk, former Chief Innovation Officer for Hyatt Hotels Corporation and current CEO of Zest Health, "When we are trying new things that are unknown or uncomfortable and are putting ourselves out there, we need to be generous."

Similarly, Jennifer Bentz, Senior Vice President of Insights and Innovation at Tyson Foods, believes praise is the fuel that energizes and stimulates group work. She adds, "As a cultural tenant in the organization, praise motivates the group and makes it okay to share ideas because people are listening and acting on them in a positive way." Praise has the power to get rid of negativity—it opens up the road to positive interaction and discovery. When optimistic energy is present, the team gets going.

Praise also nurtures innovation and exploration. We strongly believe that a culture of praise is absolutely essential for innovation to occur. The skeptic might ask, "but how is it possible to praise an uphill struggle when the chance of success is exceedingly difficult to achieve?" Innovation is burdened with possible failure and risk, and praise fuels forward-movement and lends support to the creative process itself. Getting rid of fear is essential to innovation and praise can "step in" to counter any whiff of fear. To this point, Sandee Kastrul, founder of Chicago-based i.c.stars, sees praise as an antidote to the 'culture of fear" which pervades many work settings. "There's a fear that there won't be enough, and so I need to monitor what's in his cup versus what's in mine. We end up hoarding things. If we could move past this fear of fairness there would actually be an abundance and we could get to the best possible space together." Praise, then, is non-competitive and instead helps transform a culture by nurturing and applauding risk-taking and openness to failure.

Jennifer Bentz offers a useful perspective: "I know our culture is working when I feel the energy. The energy is palpable. People are excited about what's next; they're coming in with ideas and they're willing to fail and are okay with it. People are willing to share their success stories and failures with each other to learn and grow. We get this feeling of togetherness. It's what makes me excited to be part of this culture."

Nurturing Collaborative Energy

Unless you work in complete isolation, you are always a member of some kind of team. Relationships with others are vital to success. Alone, our impact is enormously limited. Collaboration means partnership. It involves teamwork, solving tough problems, exchanging insights, sharing knowledge and communicating frustrations, joys and victories. It means leveraging the strengths of others and recognizing how best to use them towards the good of the organization. Social exchange and cooperative relationships, not isolation and competition, are keys to collaboration. It involves creating a mutually beneficial interdependency.

Innovative groups, teams and organizations need to be high-spirited and energetic. Group members are present and available to others and help them call forth their strengths. They listen — really listen. Group members help each other grow and reach their maximum potential.

Praised team members build stronger personal relationships, internally with co-workers and managers, and externally with customers, shareholders and suppliers. All of this, of course, creates a more dynamic, productive organization.

The peopleship process begins with a workplace that is meaningful and gratifying. They know they are valued members of a shared community.

Focus on the Connecting Points

Carol Bernick, retired chairman of the board of Alberto-Culver, learned early in her long career that success is achieved by having the right people around you. She postulates that leadership is defined by the ability to bring out the best in others and focus on their connecting points. We agree with her synthesis. Success comes from a well cared for collegial and collaborative team. Firing up that team requires that the right individuals are in place, their qualities are allowed to shine and they feel a strong sense of connection.

In contrast, collaboration fails if leaders choose to use others for personal gain. This outdated leadership mindset sees others as a resource for consumption. Its leaders are interested in acquiring or maintaining power. They believe, "I have the power because you don't. If others become self-empowered, then I lose power. It's either them or me." In this type of culture, collaboration does not exist. Creating a spirit of collaboration is all about instilling a mindset where people intrinsically want to help each other succeed, learn and grow.

Become a Praise Champion

"There's a kind of booby trap with growing up," observed anthropologist Mary Catherine Bateson. "The first time you use the potty properly or take a first step, everybody praises you and tells you you're wonderful. The family claps, calls grandmother, pulls out the camera and records the date. 'That's terrific! That's wonderful!' And then you walk for the rest of your life and nobody notices. In fact, they keep on commenting on the things you do wrong. Nobody says 'you've been doing good, and you're going to go on to do even better.'"

Bateson points out that what's really critical in building morale and productivity is giving team members a vision of where they're going that is positive, and a sense that they are moving. "Not a sense that they've arrived, but that there is something really exciting and worthwhile ahead of them." Leaders need to become praise change agents. They need to champion, disseminate and broadcast praise.

Praise for Curiosity and Movement Forward

Here is the core of Bateson's thinking: every action is deserving of praise in some form. Even when someone does something with awkward results, if it makes you uncomfortable or it wastes time or it proves to be a dead end, you have to praise the curiosity and effort behind it. You have to say, "That was really worth trying, and even though it didn't lead anywhere, you learned something from it."

She emphasized that you don't just praise people on the basis of results, which are not guaranteed in work—and life. You praise them on the basis of curiosity, a willingness to try and the energy that went into what may have turned out to be a dead end. It's that drive and energy that you want to reinforce, not just the actual achievement. The *character* that led to the achievement will lead to another achievement if you reinforce it. It's often useful to ask, "what led you to that idea? How did you discover that?" Rather than "the results are terrific." It's this kind of praise that works against risk aversion and convinces people to try again after failing. Don't just praise for doing something right, praise others for being curious and for taking the initiative to solve a problem on their own.

Track Accomplishments— Serve as a Resource Librarian

In addition to using specific information in praise, encourage leaders to keep track of other people's accomplishments. They should know when their team members have done something particularly well. Expert praisers can recall, for example, when their co-worker managed to share her thoughts at just the right time in the meeting, was able to remember critical details during a tight, time-crunched situation, helped find a solution to a problem or came up with a new idea. The encouraging leader knows these fine points or circumstances and can recall the necessary specific information from the team member's past.

Think of a leader as the team's "accomplishment librarian," keeping the members' past achievements within their "memory shelves." Leaders share this information with team members, provide encouragement and shout approval when necessary, and provide an extra dose of praise during difficult times of conflict and frustration. In this way, they help a team member reinforce their inner strengths, sometimes located deep within.

For example, when a team member has been criticized by someone, the encouraging leader can help identify whatever aspects might be unfair or untrue, reminding the team member of her strengths, then offering a plan that remedies the situation. If your team member is criticized for sloppy analysis, she needs to practice more on checking her findings. If told she has poor communication skills, then she needs to make more presentations or write weekly thought pieces to practice regularly sharing with her team. If told she behaves rudely, then she needs to be more considerate of others before she speaks. If a leader can think through what *specific* action needs to be taken to help the team member, then a strong and spirited co-worker can emerge.

Self-Knowledge

Ultimately, if a team member has heard over and over again that he has specific abilities and positive qualities, then the team leader is helping him believe in and further build upon his own strengths and better understand who he is. The effective team leader should be actively involved in this encouragement endeavor with all team members. This provides team members with self-knowledge by telling them, over and over, what their specific qualities are using illustrative words and descriptive-action steps. We've already discussed how hard it can be to uncover your own strengths, so leaders should do what they can to identify others' strengths for them.

Team members' self-knowledge influences every action they take. Self-evaluation can be leveraged because of the information they now have about themselves. In contrast, team members who have received no encouragement and constant negative remarks will unlikely acquire this inner positive self-knowledge. These team members are dependent on others to tell them how well they are doing, who they are and what they can do well (or not do well). When team members truly understand their unique qualities and know themselves, this provides a source of energy.

Mentor Managers On How to Give Praise

Team leaders aren't always ready to dole out praise on day one! They require some "how to" mentoring. In our interviews, we asked, "what was the most important point for senior level people to keep in mind, as it relates to praise?" Human resource pioneer, Margaret Heater, shared her perspective. "If you're given the opportunity to mentor those that are coming in behind you, ask them very openly, 'How do you see praise? Are you comfortable giving it? Do you feel that it's used too much, or that it's not genuine?' Get them to talk openly about praise and how they use it on a day-to-day basis." It's not easy to learn how to become effective and comfortable giving praise. Often managers become heavy-handed on the constructive criticism side and understate the positive attributes of a co-worker. They forget that weaving the two together is essential for learning and personal growth.

Heater believes that it's the job of senior management to make sure that they've opened up their culture to give more timely and ongoing feedback, allow their managers to grow and experience praise, and evaluate performance regularly or periodically, not annually. We completely agree. And when managers are effectively mentored, they too can become praise champions.

Praise can serve as a powerful tool to fire-up the individual, the team and the culture. Learn to nurture collaborative energy and focus on the team's connecting points. Become a praise champion. Acknowledge both curiosity and forward movement. Don't forget to mentor managers on how to give praise.

CHAPTER 10
CREATE A CULTURE OF
PRAISE AND RECOGNITION

"The more you praise and celebrate your life, the more there is in life to celebrate."
Oprah Winfrey, talk show host, actress and producer

Praise can fuel motivation, productivity and career ambition. While intangible, praise runs deep to the core. It has the power to fine-tune a person's commitment, impact and influence. Receiving constructive praise rocks the insides and motivates like no other! Praise serves as a powerful, enduring form of recognition. It also can be used to foster a culture of gratitude—a way of communicating with others to convey thankfulness for their contributions to the team and the organization.

Through our research, we were able to develop eight qualities of praise. When applied in tandem, these tactics can help leaders develop a culture of gratitude and recognition in their teams and organizations. They include:

1. View praise as an **on-going and essential ingredient** of people management.

2. Know that praise can help to make everyone in an organization **feel valued**.

3. **Personalize praise**—match the right kind and amount of praise
to each recipient.

4. Recognize the power of **indirect praise**.

5. Use **written and other tangible forms** of recognition, not just verbal praise, and give one's time too.

6. Praise **on the scene** and behind the scenes.

7. Praise both the **effort and the outcome**.

8. Create a **system for giving praise**, and be creative and consistent.

Taken together, these eight initiatives have the power to motivate personal discovery *and* contribute to the success of the team.

1. View praise as an on-going and essential ingredient of people management.

Praise is an extraordinary gift, but giving praise is not an easy task. Barbara Slater stresses: "You don't want praise to be mediocre—you want praise to have value. The value of praise comes from how it is given. There has to be sincerity and thoughtfulness behind the praise. It has to have a quality of its own." She stresses, "One can only give praise if the person giving it is comfortable with herself and can acknowledge others without being in competition with them. Giving praise is a form of love."

There is an old Native American proverb that says: "Everything that is not given is forever lost." When we help team members find ways to grow and be of service to our colleagues, we help them see the value of reaching out with praise. Let's show team members how to make a significant difference in the lives of others. Acts of kindness, service and giving praise always reward the giver as well as the receiver. They are never lost on each other.

This giving mindset says, let me give authentic praise to my team members and nurture an interest in praising and reaching out to others. Acts of praise free us from our self-imposed, me-focused lives by widening our circles of compassion. Encourage others to practice and reach out with praise. The *spirit* of giving praise transforms both the receiver and the giver. It sets up a culture that is openhearted and generous.

2. Know that praise can help to make everyone in an organization feel valued.

Nonprofit organizations often rely heavily on praise. With less recognition financially, one has to find ways to recognize or praise employees for all the good things they're doing. Aside from her lengthy career in human resources, Margaret Heater has been a non-profit volunteer for thirty years, most recently at the High Desert Museum in Bend, Oregon. "We go down to the very basic level of the organization to someone that might be feeding birds, taking care of the fish tanks or shoveling manure in the horse corral, and we ask for their opinions. We ask for them to get involved with our thought process on what the whole organization needs. We go to the most basic employee and we say 'your information counts.'" Heater makes them feel valued. That in and of itself is a form of praise, as it conveys to employees that they are an important contributor to the overall success of the organization. Similarly at the DuPage Children's Museum, another nonprofit, development officer Elaine Drikakis believes that praise encourages a more creative and innovative environment for both children and adults, making each feel valued. When all participants in an organization are praised and feel heard, the culture flourishes.

Listening is another way to demonstrate to someone that he or she is valued. Drawing from her wealth of work experience in both for-profit and nonprofit arenas, Heater shared, "Active listening is the greatest gift of praise you can give to any employee at any time. I used to love to take the most difficult employee who was having huge problems with the organization and just sit them down and say, 'What's valuable to you? What do you see in this organization that we might be missing? Help us find a way to make your position much more valuable to this company, because it means a lot to us.'" In this example, Heater describes a way to turn a negative employee around using a very specific kind of praise—one that says you are important, we care about you and we value your thoughts. Praise can make *everyone* feel valued in an organization.

3. Personalize praise—match the right kind and amount of praise to each recipient.

The way in which people are recognized for their efforts should vary. What might work for one person is not necessarily going to work with the person in the office across the corridor. Both respond to different types of incentives. Shares Orla Branigan, Marketing Director for Tec de Monterrey, "One person might prefer financial or tangible incentives, while another might respond more based on praise for their work – and somebody else may really need a deeper kind of recognition about what went on intrinsically in terms of receiving that result." Here's the crucial point: the person doing the praising must know their employees or teammates on a deep, intrinsic level to understand which forms of praise work best for *them*. The praise "giver" has to apply the praise that best suits the "receiver" to get the most out of each gesture of recognition.

Predictably, some people need praise more than others. Sam Yagan, CEO of ShopRunner and former CEO of Match Group, was asked: "How do you know when you need to give praise?" His answer: "It is either because someone has done something that warrants it, or that someone is in a state of mind where they need it." He clarifies, "I've got some people who work for me who don't seem to thrive on praise, who don't seem to need it. Maybe they're pretty secure where they are." Sam continues, "And then there are some people who need it all the time, and I think that part of being a good leader or manager is assessing when and whom and for what."

Managers have to get to know their employees on a deeper level to understand which forms of praise work best for whom. For some, praise is best communicated financially while for others it is best to use public recognition or assign new responsibilities as an acknowledgment of their growth.

Delegating high-profile and important tasks can be a welcome form of praise for certain team members. Continues Sam Yagan, "For some people the praise comes through actions. I just gave one of my senior executives a very high profile project to work on, and I think he was excited to work on it because it's an important problem. I said 'Look, this is something that everyone will know you're working on,' and that resonated with him. He is receiving this huge responsibility from the CEO to do this project that everyone knows is really important." In contrast, notes Sam, "there are some other people with whom I've been trying to get more specific in real time. I've been saying, 'Hey you did a great job in managing that meeting,' or 'Hey, thanks for correcting me.' And especially when someone does something that was risky, I try to specifically call that person out and say, 'Hey, keep doing that! Thanks for saving me in that meeting.'"

For Sam, humility plays an important role in his personalization of praise — another crucial leadership quality that we believe establishes stronger bonds with one's employees. This strengthened bond, in turn, allows a leader to better understand their employees and further improve their personalization of praise.

4. Recognize the power of indirect praise.

Not all praise gets communicated directly from manager to employee — sometimes it arrives in a more indirect fashion. This "through the grapevine" praise can be a powerful "punch" to the recipient. One interviewee, a senior executive at a consumer products company, shares several examples of being on the receiving end of this behind-your-back praise. "If I tell one of my wife's girlfriends, 'you know I just love this about my wife,' it gets back to her." In this situation, the recipient, his wife, hears the praise from others, not directly from the original giver. Nevertheless, the praise bounces forward to the person who has done something noteworthy. In a sense, praising from behind actually amplifies the praise through each of the multiple points of contact it passes.

Another example from this same executive: "I have a daughter who goes to college in New York City. I was visiting her and we went out to dinner with some friends in her small little group. They were all saying, 'Sally loves you guys; she loves you and her family.' So obviously Sally had said good things about us to them. That was more important than anything they could have posted on Facebook." This kind of behind the scenes praise was "caught" by the parents, and it made them feel good inside. When it reaches the recipient, indirect praise can provide recognition and a feeling of reward just as well. It, too, can lift people up.

5. Use written and other tangible forms of recognition, not just verbal praise, and give one's time too.

Written praise is extremely powerful. Seeing written words of praise can make the recognition "pop"—and we can go back and reread it again. It has the potential to *really* sink in. Handwritten notes or emails when someone has accomplished something can have this lasting and significant impact. Leaving a voicemail for a person who has done something well is another way to share gratitude and detail that person's contribution to the group. When they listen to it, or play it back, it becomes quite impactful. Another way to express gratitude for a job well done is to give some kind of a gift. Extraordinary over-the-top performances might warrant some kind of a monetary compensation or a dinner to express appreciation.

Giving one's personal time can also be a form of recognition. For example, Sam Yagan takes five different employees out to lunch once a month. They are the rank and file customer service reps and marketing managers who work on the line, whom he would usually never see in his normal day. He doesn't know them, but nonetheless he still spends two hours with them, and they recognize his time investment. They go back to their cubicle offices and they say, "I just had lunch with the CEO! He cares, he recognized me." Seek opportunities to spend a little one-on-one time with the people you lead; it will really mean a lot to them.

After Sam Yagan once took the entire Match.com accounting team out for lunch, they were shocked. He says, "I think the functional teams— accounting, HR, legal, IT, those kind of groups—they probably don't get praised or recognized enough. I think their output is hard to quantify; they tend to *not* generate revenue or touch customers, but they provide the backbone for the organization." This gesture didn't cost all that much in the grand scheme of things, but it brought an incredible amount of value to the employees—and that's the key! The decision of how leaders spend their time, what they talk about, the things they choose to highlight and what values they choose to emphasize are all different forms of recognition.

Effective leaders nurture a giving mindset. One such leader, Gerry Kern, former editor of the *Chicago Tribune*, used many kinds of recognition. He walked around and verbally recognized people, sent notes and gave them new work opportunities and responsibilities. On the social front, he brought in food, held receptions, bought departments drinks and took colleagues to Cubs games. While he acknowledges that one-on-one contact has more meaning, his impressive "mix" of intangible tools of recognition "lifted up" those who worked with him.

6. Praise on the scene and behind the scenes.

Large, mega endeavors and events need grandiose expressions of gratitude. They require that timely praise be given to *all* team members involved. Large events are great ways to share the limelight by giving generous credit to all who contributed to the success of the team and organization.

The EGADE Business School in Monterrey, Mexico holds an annual summit. One event was particularly well executed and delivered, as Orla Branigan detailed to us. Many people were involved in the planning of the summit, which began the *day after* the previous year's summit. To say that "*lots*" of people were involved is understating the extensive coordination required. Team members dutifully focused on everything from logistics, marketing, communications and managing speakers and agendas, to handling AV and video, pre and post communications and social media. Branigan emphasized how important it was that recognition happen immediately after the event concluded. In some cases, team members worked four days without leaving the site, and some endured through the night to make sure everything was perfect when people arrived at 7am that morning. The dean gathered the complete, albeit exhausted, team together that evening for a 'great work' speech and a round of applause for jobs well done.

The next day, there was a formal communication that went out to the entire community that recognized the achievements of the EGADE Summit, saying it had successfully met its goals, sharing details on the number of leaders that attended, as well as their discussion and debate topics. At the end of the letter, the dean recognized the entire team across the EGADE Business School who contributed in many different ways to making the event a great success. She thanked the team formally for their efforts, commitment and long hours, adding that their efforts really made a huge difference in enhancing the school's agenda locally within the business community, as well as developing and strengthening their business school throughout Mexico. What did this letter accomplish? The person who just worked thirty-six hours straight now knows that her efforts were appreciated and valued! Praise was executed both on and behind the scenes with everyone involved in the creation and execution of the event.

7. Praise both the effort and the outcome.

Each instance of giving praise is accompanied with a particular *intent*. Some praise carries the intent to create the conditions where people feel safe. For example, one might respond to a failed new product test with, "You tried that prototype and we learned that it wasn't addressing their needs." In this case, a person is talking about the effort, not the achieved outcome, prototype, behavior or generated idea. Put differently, one could have said: "That was gritty of you. You took a shot, and I want to recognize and praise you for your effort." Here, praise is for the effort — not the execution.

Those who give the praise must clarify what it is that they are recognizing. Are they rewarding efforts or achievements? Or both? It is beneficial to recognize *effort* because at a certain point, a person or a team has spent a lot of time completing a task to the best of their efforts, regardless of whether or not their endeavor was a success. This can be a very effective tool for mitigating risk aversion in a workplace culture.

If efforts are praised even when execution fails, people won't be afraid to take a risk the next time around. Other times, it's important to also link praise to the *achievement* of specific goals. We think recognition and praise has enormous value in both situations—when it is directly connected to efforts and to tangible achievements.

8. Create a system for giving praise, and be creative and consistent.

Praise and acknowledgement are unquestionably important for any culture or organization, and when there is a "system" in place, the two flow more easily and organically. Shares Brian Bannon, Commissioner of the Chicago Public Libraries: "Praise and acknowledgement are key, but in our organization we haven't yet created a system. While independently our mangers and leaders value praise and acknowledgement as part of the culture, I don't think we have established systems that let us know it's happening." Putting such a system in place to guarantee that praise is executed is a great idea, but it can be very difficult to institute such a stark shift in the status quo.

Here are four established systems that we discovered in our interviews, which help team leaders and members both give and receive recognition publicly and showcase their appreciation.

1. *The Grow Awards*—"Our employees are incentivized to engage in innovation through a performance goal built into their performance metrics. Individuals are recognized for coming up with ideas. Called the Grow Awards, it is a system where anyone can recognize anyone else publicly and showcase that appreciation. People are recognized by their peers for their ideas or for advancing the culture of the company. Employees accumulate points, and they can buy items through a catalog. There are different award levels and each "winner" is published on an Internet page for all to see." Jennifer Bentz, CIO of Tyson Foods

2. *Mad Props*—Employees at Pete Kadens' former firm, SoCore Energy, created a platform called "Mad Props" as a way to drive a culture of recognition. Throughout the month, people submit

compliments that must adhere to what an employee did well in the workplace. These compliments are submitted to and administered by a central repository. Management is not allowed to participate in Mad Props. At year-end, all compliments are quantified and the employee with the most "Mad Props" wins a cash prize. The largest gifts were for $15,000 cash, then $7,500 and $2,500. In the end, each Mad Prop winner goes on a wall of fame.

3. *Annual Awards Dinner*—Given their patent-focused culture, employees at Cleversafe created a unique system of recognition. Anyone who received a patent during the year is given an award. When employees receive their tenth patent award, winners are recognized and receive plaques, shared Chris Gladwin, founder and CEO.

4. *Academy Awards*—Employees at SMS Assist put in place their own unique academy awards to provide peer recognition. Chairman and CEO Michael Rothman and CFO Marc Shiffman stressed that these awards were for *everyone* at all levels. They are "creative" Academy Awards, made from their training videos. The "movie" actors are all SMS Assist employees who play different roles in the videos. Ceremoniously, the company gives out unique Academy Awards to all the "actors." Imagine the fun—and recognition—that occurs at this event!

In short, praise needs to become an ongoing management tool that is tracked and measured. It needs to occur often enough that it can be infused in the company culture and reach everyone at an organization, and it also needs to be tailored and specified to the person (or people) it is targeted to so it is right for them.

Set up a culture of gratitude by practicing the eight praised-based initiatives.

SECTION

2

UNLEASH THE
LEADER WITHIN

CHAPTER 11
IDENTIFY STRENGTHS WITHIN YOURSELF AND OTHERS

"What lies behind us and what lies before us are small matters compared to what lies within us."

Ralph Waldo Emerson, essayist, lecturer and poet

Many people fear the dreaded job interview. It's stressful, intimidating and often high-stakes. Preparation for a big interview can mean extensive company and industry research, memorizing a good "elevator pitch," and sometimes even buying a new suit or dress. But one thing that is common among all interviews is the infamous question, "tell me about your strengths and weaknesses." Most of us know in which areas we struggle or need improvement, though that won't stop us from making up fake weaknesses that really sound good such as, "I work too hard" or "I'm a perfectionist." When it comes to talking about our strengths, on the other hand, for some reason many of us struggle with describing in detail what we are best at.

Ask yourself if you know your top three strengths. List them right now. Do they surface easily or are they difficult to define? Many people aren't truly aware of their strengths or they tend to downplay them. Defining our strengths and really knowing what we are great at enables us to build on these assets and leverage them even more. Also, by understanding what we are best at, we are able to better identify what we need to improve on. Sadly, people often end up focusing on their perceived weaknesses and their development needs rather than where they excel.

Calling Out Our Strengths and Leveraging Them

To unleash the leader within, the first step requires that we identify and understand our strengths. Understanding one's own strengths and being able to leverage them is an absolute necessity, otherwise a person is unable to differentiate themself from their peers. How can someone expect to be viewed as extraordinary or deserving of praise if they don't know what they are best at?

Sandee Kastrul is the president and co-founder of Chicago-based i.c.stars, a technology-based workforce leadership and development program for low-income young adults. She eloquently stresses that we have to "stand out where we are really good, less we get whipped around by the wind." She feels that if we are unable to identify and leverage our strengths or comparative niche, we will be overshadowed by those that can.

If you feel as though you are someone who has difficulty with introspection and identifying your own strengths, don't fear. An extremely valuable source for recognizing your skills is praise from others. As a life-long student and practitioner in the personal development space, even Sandy Kastrul relies on others to help her zero-in on what makes her special. Kastrul shared: "I need praise because we do extraordinary things every day, but these will become ordinary if we don't call them out." Praise gives others a chance to communicate to us what they perceive to be our strengths, and this external confirmation works to solidify our self-confidence and gives praise a home.

Being aware of your strengths enables you to leverage them, as well as build on or compensate for areas where you are weaker. The journey to finding your strengths can be difficult, but once completed it can be very powerful. As Sam Yagan puts it, "you need to find your comparative advantage; you have to find the thing you are good at." He discussed how he discovered his strength and affinity for teaching while at Harvard University, and leveraged that to surmount his relative shortcomings among his peers: "Even though I was by far the worst computer scientist of the thirty teaching assistants, I won 'Teacher of the Year' six of the seven semesters. Everyone else knew the underlying material better than I did, but I was able to explain it well. I had empathy for the students because I also struggled with the material." Through the praise and recognition of his teaching skills, Sam discovered several unique characteristics or strengths within himself and was able to leverage them to stand out among his peers.

Becoming Visible

Your combination of strengths makes you unique—and makes you visible. Picture an artist's palette with globs of different colored paints in a semi-circle. Each color on the palette represents a particular strength or skill, and how the artist decides to utilize each of them is an active choice. With brush in hand, the artist is ready to mix the paints together and apply them to the canvas. But before the artist begins, he looks closely at the individual colors and considers multiple combinations.

Do you know what makes you visible—your colors? You must learn to value and appreciate your strengths and advantages. Knowing who you are and what your strengths are can help to identify activities for personal growth. What do you want to achieve, learn, acquire and master in the workplace? How can you find ways to achieve your personal goals? The workplace can become a pathway to enable personal development and growth. Each individual characteristic and need can be matched with at least one activity or action. These become our individual growth goals and plans.

Quit hiding your treasures; present them in the everyday life of your workplace. Find your creative voice deep inside. Give yourself space to excel. Take time to explore and express. Develop all your skills, from the intuitive to the technical. Nurture your unique gifts. With enough work and growth, you can illuminate your entire organization.

Discovering the Self

There are four ways to explore and discover "Who am I?"

1. Get in touch with your personal values.

A value is something that is important to you. It defines who you are, what you believe in and what you cherish. Values influence the choices we make, the way we invest our energy and time, the people we choose to be close to and the interests we pursue. In difficult times, they serve as a compass amid conflicting demands and varying points of view. To lay a foundation for a life that is meaningful and satisfying, you must know exactly what your personal values are.

What are my values? Write down 5 to 10 of your own personal values—whatever you believe in. Although this identification process might sound simple, it requires some serious thought and reflection. Recognize the intrinsic worth, strengths and merit of your values.

Understanding your personal values creates greater harmony in a group. While there is often overlap, every person has a unique set of values and principles. Disconnect with or contradiction of another person's values can cause conflict, and this is especially true when a person isn't open about their values. When a team shares their values or makes them apparent, there is an awareness of what's important to each group member. You can use this information to improve your working relationship with others, as well as plan what to do with your own work time, free time, weekends and vacations in order to tap into your primary interests.

2. Get in touch with your personal characteristics and needs.

Take that same piece of paper where you wrote down your values, and below them note the characteristics that best answer these two questions "Who am I?" and "What are my professional needs?" Do some deep thinking on this, and keep your previously answered values in mind – if you find yourself making changes to your previous list that is a good thing! Write at least three qualities that best describe your individual traits and needs.

3. Take a close look at your strengths and improvement areas.

Be up front and personal when you take a look at your strengths and improvement areas. It is important to recognize the things you do well and don't do well so you can recognize how they interact with others and reflect the needs of a group.

To get started, use the checklist of questions below to expand your thinking and consider new areas of growth and development. Think about each question definitively as it relates to a strength or an improvement area.

- Do I communicate openly by expressing my own feelings and emotions?
- Do I take risks?
- Do I suggest ideas that I believe might promote the achievement of the group's goals?
- Do I actively listen?
- Am I sensitive and empathetic to individual needs?
- Do I help others experience success?
- Do I frequently use descriptive praise?
- Do I ask for feedback on how well I am communicating and interacting with each group member?
- Do I stimulate self-initiated growth and personalized learning?
- Do I give sufficient freedom to learn?
- Do I frequently use humor?
- Do I ask group members how I could improve?
- Do I stimulate creative and intuitive thinking?

Finally, complete the strengths and weaknesses exercise by answering these four questions:

1. What are my three greatest strengths?

2. What are three areas in which I'd like to improve?

3. "I disappoint members of the group when I…."

4. "I can really motivate a group member when I…."

4. Explore the factors that have shaped your values.

Change can be rampant, wild and unpredictable, much like Alice shared in Lewis Carroll's *Alice in Wonderland*: "Who Are You?," said the caterpillar. Alice replied rather shyly, "I…I hardly know sir, just at present—at least I know who I was when I got up this morning, but I must have changed several times since then."

Values evolve over time in response to the forces of life. Some of these forces are stubborn and relentless. Others are sudden, almost shattering. Still others are so gentle and subtle that we scarcely notice them. Think about your own values. What are their origins? How have they changed?

Four factors usually shape our values: (1) family and childhood experiences, (2) personal relationships with significant individuals, (3) major life changes and learning experiences and (4) conflict events that produce self-discovery. Combined with our own learning, these factors transform our values over time. Let's take a closer look at each to see its impact on our values.

1. ***Family and childhood experiences.*** During childhood, parents, family members, siblings, peers, teachers, and religious and community organizations share their beliefs and, in turn, shape our values. The goal of a good parent or role model is to impart onto youth what they believe to be positive values so that they can grow up to be upstanding citizens themselves. Our childhood experiences from school, family rituals, holidays and celebrations, travel and vacations, as well as daily family life all work together to form our core values.

2. ***Personal relationships with significant individuals.*** There are a handful of individuals that we meet in our lives who really "connect"

with us. Teachers, classmates, bosses, coworkers or friends can all be special role models whom we look up to, respect, admire and try to emulate. As we become close with them and form a more intimate relationship, their core values become more apparent to us. The stronger the bond, the more their values influence the formation and evolution of our own.

3. *Major life changes and learning experiences.* Marriage, rearing children, taking a new job or position, moving to a new location, confronting the death of a significant other or adjusting to the departure of children from home all cause our values to shift and evolve over time. Dealing with significant life changes means making important values-based decisions. Discovering new motivations, emotions and conflicts within ourselves can bring new light to old beliefs that we have always taken for granted, or bring to light values we hold but never before realized. Learning more about ourselves, dealing with different kinds of people and experiencing new things invites us to examine and reinvent our values.

4. *Conflict events.* Conflict often transforms our values in deep and lasting ways. There is an endless list of conflict events in one's life. Going to war, losing a job, divorcing a spouse or failing at a new business are all examples of conflict events that can cause a shift in one's values. When this happens, we need to be self-aware and adjust our set of values to include whatever new ones emerge.

Your Star Quality

What makes you a star? Each of us has what we call "star quality." It requires self-awareness, a close look at "Who am I?" and "What are my professional needs?" Once we truly grasp what this means, we can shine our beams of light proudly and brightly. Life is full of forces that cause us to examine and reexamine our values. Discovering how our values are shaped provides greater insight into who we are and what we might become. While each of the above four factors can transform our values, they can never be fully understood until they are examined through introspection.

Turn On the Bright Light of Others

You've become visible by knowing your strengths. You're a high-watt bulb coping in a low-watt bulb workplace. What about your colleagues? How do they get out of their low-watt world? How can their light shine brighter so they won't get lost too?

Employees must expand their self-knowledge, but most people can't do this on their own. They must have help or encouragement in becoming aware of their strengths and needs. Earlier in this chapter we learned how to decipher our own individual strengths—our unique colors, from the mixed palate that is our personality. Good leaders and colleagues should try to help un-mix the colors of others in the workplace. As leaders, it is important to maintain and encourage this double focus. Besides asking, "who am I?" we must also know or have an answer for "who are you?"

Know the Characteristics and Needs of Others in the Group

As group members, we must learn to do things for others. A group is only as strong as its individual members, so strengthening others strengthens the whole. To start this group building process, identify and understand the strengths and needs of each co-worker. Begin by assessing the unique strengths for each colleague in the group by asking and discussing what makes them distinctive, what are their strong points and what makes them different from others. Gradually, we learn what each person brings to the group. A team can be built that reflects the collective needs of the organization.

Leaders may try to impose their own strengths and needs onto their employees instead of learning what each employee brings to the culture of the workplace. It is important to understand and be sensitive to all fellow workers. We should become aware of each of their characteristics and needs, and get to know them well. Greater wattage or light can only occur when everyone's strengths and needs are powered up and made more visible.

Just like a beautiful painting emerges from the mix of colors, a workplace offers an opportunity for a remarkable piece of art to emerge. In a nurturing culture, employees will show their strengths and express their needs. They will grow and develop individually, and nourish one another too. An imaginative painting begins to form from the mix of colors.

Appreciate the Different Kinds of Intelligence

There is a magical quality to the study of intelligence, if we broaden our definition of it; everyone is smart—just in different ways. Leaders must understand that there are different kinds of intelligence. An IQ score measures intelligence with words and numbers. It provides the traditional definition of ability. It says a co-worker is smart if she can read a problem and understand what happened, or do advanced numerical calculations with ease. Standardized scores reflect these more traditional types of intelligence, but such tests actually restrict the definition of intelligence.

Ask yourself if you think of these people as intelligent: The technician who quickly identified why your computer wouldn't work, the speaker who kept the group laughing with engaging stories, the friend who can understand why you feel the way you do before you share your thoughts or the co-worker who can play four instruments and quickly sing a new song by just looking at the musical score. The truth is that <u>all</u> of these people are smart, but they express their intelligence differently.

Howard Gardner, co-director of Project Zero at Harvard University, has broadened intelligence to include *nine* areas:

1. **Bodily-kinesthetic intelligence ("Body Smart")**, which means demonstrating coordination, ability and skill in both fine and gross motor movements, as with a craftsperson or athlete.

2. **Existential intelligence ("Cosmic Smart")**, means sensitivity and capacity to tackle deep questions about human existence like the meaning of life, why do we die and how did we get here.

3. **Interpersonal intelligence or social ability ("People Smart")**, which means having a strong ability to enjoy friends and groups and their activities; they excel at perceiving people's moods, temperaments, motivations and intentions as well as displaying empathy.

4. **Intrapersonal intelligence ("Self Smart")**, which means being deeply aware of one's own feelings and thoughts, and being able to recognize and discriminate among these feelings. These people are aware of what they love and fear, are able to insightfully talk about their own experiences and have an unusually keen understanding of themselves.

5. **Linguistic intelligence ("Word Smart")**, which means using language to communicate written and spoken meanings—to write and read at a superior level. It also includes being able to wordplay, rhyme, tell stories and enjoy puns.

6. **Logic-mathematical intelligence ("Number/Reasoning Smart")**, which means thinking conceptually, reasoning, devising experiments, exploring abstract relationships in math, computers and logic, and noticing patterns and numbers in their environment.

7. **Musical intelligence ("Music Smart")**, which means being able to sing on key, maintain a beat, remember music that has been heard or compose and read songs.

8. **Naturalist intelligence ("Nature Smart")**, which means discriminating among living things (plants, animals) and the natural world (clouds, rock formations). Valuable to hunters, gatherers and farmers in our evolutionary past, and central in roles such roles as botanist or chef today.

9. **Spatial intelligence ("Picture Smart")**, which means having good visual memory or the ability to find one's way around, read maps, take things apart and reassemble them, or work with paints, design, light or architectural drawings.

Taken together, these types of intelligence provide nine ways to learn. They broaden our definition of intelligence, and in so doing, free a team member to be intelligent from several different perspectives. Leaders must learn what kind of intelligence their co-workers have in order to nurture and strengthen them.

Understanding the characteristics and professional needs of each group member is a prerequisite for managing a team of people effectively. Without this knowledge, one could end up leading in the dark.

Become visible – know your strengths and call them out and share them. Identify which "beams of light" makes you a star. Know the characteristics and needs of others in the group. Identify each team member's strengths and intelligence types so everyone can develop personalized goals and visions.

CHAPTER 12
BECOME AN ACTIVE AND
ENTHUSIASTIC LEADER

"I have no special talents. I am only passionately curious."

**Albert Einstein, theoretical physicist
who developed the theory of relativity**

Leaders with professional passion convey excitement, warmth and emotion in everything that they do, ranging from how they speak to how they act. This energizing passion serves as a catalyst for breathing enthusiasm into a values-based culture. Leaders can help employees get excited about their work, take pride in their jobs and feel emotionally committed to their colleagues. We feel that expressing emotion, rather than suppressing it, should become a new leadership norm.

Effective leaders constantly re-energize the work force in order to make organizations more productive, competitive and ultimately profitable. By instilling group-developed norms and values to guide individual behavior, a "values fabric" can be created to provide shared group expectations within the entire organization.

Paying Attention

In our in-depth interview with prominent cultural anthropologist Mary Catherine Bateson, she emphasized: "What's valuable is a sense that somebody that I work with or work for is paying attention to what I'm doing and spontaneously saying 'you're on the right track.'" Correctly, "You're on the right track" is very different from "you did a good job." The first response not only provides praise but has built in the expectation that you're going to do more and better, while the second response suggests closure. Additionally, "You're on the right track," embraces a sense of excitement for the future or a "the best is yet to come" kind of feeling, which is vastly different from excitement about what's been done in the past.

Here's an essential element to this discovery: in order to observe that a team member is heading in the appropriate direction, lots and lots of active watching and paying attention are required.

Bateson goes on to say that when you are engaged like this, watching intensely, you're witnessing someone on the "edge of growth." She stressed, "You're not looking at the failures because they discourage you, you're looking at the growth and you're ready for more." Now this is an exciting place to be for *both* people involved.

Leaders must look for and get to know the positive attributes of each person on their team. By paying close attention, they can help their team members see, respect and value their own inner strengths. We think this is their most important job. But how do you help your team member see her bright colors, her unique strengths? *Reflect back what you see.* Then communicate it to them.

The Value of Positive Affirmation

Affirmations or statements of praise are powerful ways to reflect back what you see—and the more specific, the better. Most praise is too general and because of this, it doesn't build self-esteem. Many leaders will simply say, "You worked hard" or "You did a terrific job." Their praise is generic; they've forgotten to add any specific information. When praise becomes specific, employees get more than just insights into what they did well—they see that their leader cares and is paying attention. A team member needs to hear that she is wonderful, *and why*.

Put a WOW in your voice and applaud with enthusiasm. Try out a new level of enthusiasm now. The difference in its impact will totally surprise you! If a team member has done an extraordinary job, give a round of applause or a standing ovation. Affirmations are not something given occasionally or on a part-time basis, but continuously—every chance you get. Don't wait to extend your praise; give it quickly or soon after it is due, and always remember that it needs to be authentic and genuine.

Each team member has qualities inside him or her that need to be pointed out. It may take this form: "Henry, I love working with you because you have a funny sense of humor. I feel you bring innovative thinking to the group, you are very observant and have strong people instincts, and I learn more when you're around!" Now what happens to this team member if he is told—frequently—that he makes you laugh, is creative, communicates openly, has good insight into people and acts as a teacher? If he hears it over and over from a superior and potential role model, he is more likely to absorb and really appreciate this information. People who know their strengths, who are aware of their unique qualities, become stronger and more confident. The ultimate goal is for a team member to be secure in her own abilities and no longer be dependent on the opinion of others. This person can say, "I do these things well," and believe it!

Managing Learning—Start With Self-Discovery

An impactful leader plays the role of a Socratic teacher. It is someone to help you manage your personal learning, draw out information and guide self-discovery. It is not a small job! The goal is to give employees the tools to help them improve themselves, as opposed to spoon-feeding them what to do. The learner is the most important person in the process—not the teacher or leader. The leader helps the learner integrate information into a real-world context or application in the form of skills, techniques or knowledge.

We believe the four stages of managing learning are:

1. *Self-Discovery*—the teacher does lots of listening to find out what a person already knows before sharing information or trying to "teach" something. This is the most important step in the learning process. By asking a series of questions, the learner is

self-assessing what is known and unknown about a certain topic or skill. This gap or space becomes the starting point for learning to begin. It is the critical vantage point. Without it, a teacher doesn't know what to focus on.

2. *Instruction*—new material is "presented" to the learner and customized according to which modes of learning are best received by the learner. Modes to choose from include hearing, seeing, experiencing, writing and doing.

3. *Application*—the learner is given a chance to try out or use the newly acquired skill or information, and inform the leader if learning has occurred. This application of learning is essential for it to "stick" over time.

4. *Evaluation*—Learners find out for themselves and evaluate what they have learned and how well they executed it. In the managing learning process, the learners take responsibility for their own growth. The onus is on them—not the teacher. Once evaluation has occurred, this new learning becomes part of the self-discovery knowledge base.

This managing learning process serves as a tool for better observation, integration and absorption of information. If you don't have one in place, find a team member or leader to serve as a helper or Socratic teacher and get ready to discover, teach, apply and evaluate.

Have passion for your work and express it. Build your team member's confidence with lots of specific and enthusiastic feedback. Formalize the "managing learning" process.

CHAPTER 13
ENCOURAGE CREATIVITY
AND CONFLICT

"Conflict is the gadfly of thought. It stirs us to observation and memory. It instigates to invention. It shocks us out of sheeplike passivity, and sets us at noting and contriving."

John Dewey, American philosopher, psychologist and educational reformer

Thomas Edison had a unique means of capturing his unconventional ideas while relaxing in his special napping chair. It was large, comfortable and had good-sized arm rests. Before napping, he would put ball bearings in his hands and two pie plates on the floor. He kept a note pad on his lap. Whenever he fell asleep, the ball bearings would drop on the pie plates and wake him up. He would jot down some notes on what was passing through his mind at the time, then fall back to sleep. This was his imaginative way of catching theta-waves, which are brain-waves rich in creativity. Theta waves are full of ideas and often lead to fresh perceptions and thoughts. Adults can only experience them in a sleep stage psychologists call "hypnagogia," or the borderlands between wakefulness and rest. It is a fascinating state of consciousness characterized by dream-like visions and strange sensory occurrences.

It is wild to think that electricity may have been discovered through the process of napping! If you really want to nurture more creativity, consider adding a comfortable couch to each office. Attach a clipboard or "think pad" to it. W. Clement Stone, the founder of Combined Insurance which today is known as Aon Insurance, used a bathtub that he called his "think tank" to generate new ideas. He kept a small blackboard nearby to jot down his creative thoughts while relaxing in the tub.

Whether it's dozing off in a comfy chair or soaking in the tub, it would do us all good to find the environments in which we are the most intuitive and creative.

Generate Bold Ideas

Picture the following small team: Seven people together discussing a pressing topic, all of whom are in relative agreement except one who is going in a completely unique and unusual direction. He immediately stands out of the group. He is not following the others. We can easily see that he is expressing something rare and exceptional—a creative solution to the problem at hand.

How many times have you been in a group and had a creative idea but didn't let it out? You didn't raise your hand and express it, even though you wanted to, because you weren't sure if it would be accepted by the group. Perhaps this happens to you frequently. Or, maybe you don't have any creative ideas anymore, because they aren't really encouraged in your workplace's culture. Maybe you are afraid to share your ideas aloud for fear of being told they have been tried in the past and didn't work.

Bold and game-changing ideas are potent. They have the power to nourish and ignite the workplace and can greatly contribute to the organization's future strength and growth. So how can we encourage more fresh idea sharing in the workplace culture? Most importantly, the leaders and managers have to want it. They have to say "YES" to it. They must give their employees the freedom to take risks and play with ideas. This requires a new type of leader, one that encourages employees to connect with their creative potential and actually use their intuition.

Know and remind yourself that creativity can be nurtured and even taught in the workplace. Importantly, we need to value intuition; it is the key to creativity. Simply put, intuition means letting go of our over-analytical thinking mind and getting in touch with our inner feelings. At the same time, it calls for a sense of trust in the abilities of our unconscious mind. We must trust and accept it in its natural, unorganized state. The task for the unconscious mind is to take an assortment of "stuff"—collected information—and organize it into something entirely new, even unanticipated. Intuition, then, involves learning to let go, trusting the unconscious mind to make sense of all the collected "data" and staying open to the ideas and discoveries that surface.

Praise Generously to Stimulate Innovation

Praise creates a safe environment where people can think, learn, explore, innovate and try new things. Jeff Semenchuk, currently CEO of Zest Health, shared a personal experience at one of Hyatt's Global Leadership Summits, a gathering of every general manager from over 600 hotels and 100 senior executives. He had volunteered for a fun exercise: The large group was told that every time Jeff did something, they were to applaud wildly and cheer loudly. He then was given a small box on stage. When he opened the box, the crowd became thunderous and started clapping. He shared, "I was feeling all sorts of affirmation, which was of course the lesson—that we need to praise and get support. When we are trying new things that are unknown or uncomfortable and putting ourselves out there, we need to be generous." Praise is especially important in the innovation process, he notes, "if someone says, 'that's a stupid idea,' no one wants to put an idea out there a second time."

Kristi Lafleur, the former CEO of the Illinois Tollway, also believes that praise plays a powerful role in the innovation process. "People *need* to be acknowledged for the good work that they do, especially when they take risks and push the envelope." Jennifer Bentz, Tyson Foods VP of Consumer Insights and Strategy, concurs: "Praise is really important in shaping an innovation culture. It gives the organization the opportunity to tell people they've done a good job. It's a cultural tenant in the organization, and I think it motivates people and makes it okay to share ideas because people are listening and acting on those ideas."

Make Use of Conflict

Conflict is an ordinary part of group work. The effective leader must know how to deal with all kinds of conflict in a group setting. What's the best approach? Try to resolve the conflict as soon as possible—right? Not necessarily. Instead, let the group members experience conflict. Most leaders' gut reaction is to act as mediators and step in to quickly resolve the conflict, but by doing that they rob their group members of the valuable experience of learning to deal with the conflict themselves.

To our critical point, groups whose leaders halt conflict are not allowing for individual growth. Conflict serves as a catalyst for the group member to take total responsibility for resolving the situation. If the manager mediates, this opportunity is lost.

One of the reasons small groups often function better than large groups is because heightened conflict and intense disorganization are easier to resolve in smaller settings. There is more room for everyone's voice to be heard, and so a more reasonable discourse can be had. We have found that people are much more likely to listen to and sympathize with a conflicting argument when they feel that they have had their opinions heard as well.

Once the leader and group members have developed a powerful sense of community through shared values, a sense of ownership and common goals, each individual within the team will feel more empowered to go against the grain and throw out a game-changing idea. Ironically, the security and closeness of a team actually encourages conflict; team members know that they can risk sharing a fresh idea, and if it isn't well received that conflict will quickly disseminate. A team that is well-versed in conflict resolution is one that allows for risk-taking and innovation to test the limits of what is possible. Conversely, when group dynamics are such that a "bad" idea is met with aggression and conflict that is not easily resolved, team members in the future will be hesitant to risk upsetting the status quo.

Balance Team Building and Conflict

Maintaining a strong sense of community with a team requires leaders and members to be concerned with its perpetuation, growth and prosperity. Any event or activity can serve to maintain and build a stronger sense of belonging, especially when it involves opportunities to challenge, create conflict and then resolve it.

So, to make use of conflict, remind yourself of these five qualities of effective groups:

1. *Participative*—there is active involvement and engagement in dialogue, actions and decisions from all members

2. *Supportive*—members are respectful of others and their points-of-view; they are encouraging and empathetic of colleagues' ideas and suggestions

3. *Informal leadership*—leaders and members alike are agile and quick to step in and offer input and information

4. *Small in size*—a team size is generally most effective when between five and ten individuals at most

5. *Informal in structure*—there is little or no hierarchy, nor elaborate reporting relationships and structure

Participative, supportive and small groups facilitate a sense of ownership, develop trust in others and build personal relationships. Informality and encouragement allow for members to experience conflict. Part of the natural course of any group dynamic is conflict—listening for agreement and disagreement, working through differences and inconsistencies, and reaching a point of understanding and compromise. Leadership skills are learned from this "messy" process.

Engage in Constructive Confrontation

There is often the tendency for team members to avoid direct confrontations or conflicts in the workplace. As a consequence, there is often a substantial amount of uncertainty regarding team member performance. Without candid feedback and criticism, how can someone possibly be expected to grow? Team members truly want to know "where they stand." It's that simple. They expect confrontation and criticism, especially when fellow team members or co-workers are underperforming or negatively impacting the effectiveness of the team.

Despite its inherent uncomfortable nature, conflict can be constructive. It can stir up growth. While at times it may take us one step back, when resolved it moves the whole team two steps forward.

Encourage, nurture and value creativity and bold game-changing ideas. While counterintuitive, know that conflict is a good experience for teams. Don't be the instant mediator. Use conflict to guide progress and understand why we lose ground.

CHAPTER 14
PRESENT ENERGETICALLY AND EXPRESS YOURSELF EMOTIONALLY

"The expressiveness of the individual appears to involve two radically different kinds of activity: the expression that he gives, and the expression that he gives off."

Erving Goffman, considered the most influential American sociologist of the twentieth century

Picture this: A person is speaking to a group of people sitting around a circular table. His audience's eyes are glazed, their shoulders are slouched and no one is taking notes or asking questions. This is often a shared experience in the business world. In this group, everyone is profoundly bored. Though their eyes might be open, not one person is awake. Several heads are resting on the table, and others have fallen back to sleep on their chairs. But despite all this, the presenter is still talking—even using body language to communicate his message. Unfortunately, he is the only one who is alert. No listening is occurring; information is not being exchanged.

The Key Tenants of Enthusiastic Presentation

Presentation skills are essential for getting others to listen to what you are saying and engage others in meaningful discussion. How information is presented is key to successful discussion and decision-making. Good speakers know that it is critical to keep the group fired-up and alive. The presenter must open up, share ideas, convey warmth and interest, learn the needs of the group and apply this knowledge to help them grow and rally together.

Talking to a group of people is a skill for everyone to master. Ron Hoff's *I Can See You Naked: A Fearless Guide to Making Great Presentations* is a great book on this subject. Presentations offer a unique and rare opportunity to present ourselves in a way that is closer to our real selves than our everyday work selves. Unfortunately, this doesn't happen very often because most presenters rarely let their guards down. Ron Hoff describes a classic example of this: "The presenter scrunches down behind the podium so no one can see him, reads from his script so he will say nothing spontaneous, keeps his eyes down so that no one can make eye contact, and holds his voice monotone at one deadly level to muffle his emotions. No fun." Mr. Hoff dedicates his book to the exhilaration of presenting well and the feeling of joy that accompanies it. If everyone practiced what he prescribes, these "bored rooms" would soon disappear.

The best parts of his how-to-present guide are Hoff's "nuggets". There are four that can make a significant impact when trying to keep a group or team fired-up. *First*, view your presentation as a large, buoyant exercise ball. You know, the kind that you blow up and use for a work out. You must guide it, tap it higher, even hit it with your head if necessary. Move it around a lot and get the audience involved but know that it must always come back to you. You must keep it "alive" because it is your ball. The ball represents energy. The person who is talking needs to convey dynamism, verve, enthusiasm, vivacity, gusto, punch or spirit. Most certainly, the audience wants and needs this energy to stay attentive. It is the speaker's responsibility to keep it alive and in the air at all times.

A *second nugget*: try to use what Hoff calls "perfect moments," or a dramatic moment or climax in the presentation that causes everyone to rally around the speaker or idea. If you can work them into your presentation, you will capture the audience, communicate on a higher level, bring emotional closeness and ignite the group. They will feel as if they have shared an inspirational or uplifting experience that leaves an everlasting impression. For example, when we teach on the topic of how to listen compassionately, we ask two students to throw a Frisbee back and forth in front of the class. Awkward for many to throw and catch, Frisbee tossing perfectly conveys our point: to catch a thought we must pay attention, focus on the thrower, anticipate where it is going to be thrown and finally make the catch. Deep listening and Frisbee throwing require complementary skills and efforts of both speaker and listener. Tossing the Frisbee dramatically teaches team members the skills involved in compassionate listening—plus they are left with a lasting impression. This is quite the contrast from the picture of the timid script reader, hurrying to complete his ideas and leaving the entire audience itching to leave.

A *third nugget* from Mr. Hoff: Don't just go up and present a case, build a lasting relationship with each person in the room. They are there to hear you openly share your knowledge, ideas, talent and wisdom. You should offer a heartfelt desire to help them. Warm up an audience with frequent and friendly eye contact. Then, open up, don't hunker down; share what you know rather than guard what you don't. And, respect your audience. The "presentation" according to Hoff is just that simple.

A *final nugget*: the presenter must always remember that the best presentations are all about the audience. This means to start with an issue that is concerning to the audience. Then apply your knowledge in a strategic way to help them see their problem differently. Add evidence, offer a resolution—an idea, plan, product or package, and identify its benefits. Importantly, suggest specific next steps for them to take. Remember, audiences always have their self-interests in mind. They want the presenter to talk about them using their language and they want to leave knowing that the time spent was worthwhile.

If the focus of the presenter is on keeping the ball up, sharing perfect moments, building relationships and focusing on the audience's needs, even the most apathetic of audiences will be engaged. The key tenants of good presentation skills mirror many of the best practices we recommend for organizations trying to nurture a positive, innovative culture.

First, the culture must be alive; everyone must help keep the ball up. Second, the group needs to unite or rally around shared "perfect experiences," whether it's a trip to celebrate a good year or a difficult group rebuilding period after a failed experiment or launch. Third, open up and build lasting personal relationships with each of your fellow colleagues. Convey warmth, respect and genuine interest in them. Finally, know their needs and apply your knowledge strategically to these concerns and issues. If you do these things in your workplace, boredom will be replaced by enthusiasm. No one will want to take a nap. Everyone will be all fired-up.

Express Yourself to Create Emotional Connection

There is a different kind of "presentation" that also requires active attention and growth: your own presence—or the image that you give off. Presence, as social psychologists describe it, is the image or persona we build around ourselves and display to the rest of the world. It is akin to wearing a mask of an actor that we portray in the everyday life of the workplace. The problem with masks is that we lose the ability to see beyond them. We are also prevented from deeply experiencing many of life's fortunes because we are so focused on preserving the mask itself. In the workplace, masks keep us from getting to know the people we interact with on a daily basis. Our goal should be to let our genuine presence shine and be our true selves.

Face Work Versus Self-Work

Erving Goffman studied human behavior in social situations and the way we appear to others in his book *The Presentation of Self in Everyday Life*. He used the metaphor of theatrical performance as a framework. He believed that when an individual comes in contact with others, that person will attempt to control or guide the impression that others might make of him by changing or fixing his setting, appearance and manner.

Goffman affirmed that all participants in social interactions share a common primary goal of attempting to avoid being embarrassed or embarrassing others. Using his dramaturgical analysis, Goffman saw a connection between theatrical performances and the kinds of acts that people perform in their daily lives. In social interaction, like in theatrical performance, there is a foremost region where the "actors" (individuals) are on stage in front of their audience. This is where the positive aspects of the idea of self and desired impressions are highlighted. It is where people display what they most want others to see and focus their attention. But there also is a hidden or private place "back stage" where individuals can be themselves regardless of their role or identity in society. For us, we want group interaction to be where the self shines bright, where members are expressing who they really are.

The Power of Two-way Communication

Everyone has to work together to keep a team's bond healthy, but this is easier said than done. It requires constant open communication with ample compassion. If you are down on somebody because you are not happy with that person's performance, and you don't talk with them about it, then you get stuck in a toxic environment. When the communication is strong, the bond becomes stronger. If even one team member gets left out or doesn't participate for whatever reason, the bond is impacted. To prevent this from happening, team members must learn to talk deeply and reach out. When they do, strengthened relationships and deepened bonds emerge.

Learning how to talk to one another is the single most important thing we can do to create a strong team. Imagine what a team environment would be like if there was no talking. This happens most often in strict teams where members are afraid to say anything, so they remain silent. Communication gaps exist in most teams, and communication that is honest and respectful can be rare. Yelling—the worst form of communication—should of course be forbidden. Healthy teams are built through frequent, careful two-way communication.

The Energy of Openness

Talk can be a powerful tool from day one. Haim Ginott, author of *Teacher and Child*, said: "How parents and teachers talk tells a child how they feel about him. Their statements affect his self-esteem and self-worth. To a large extent, their language determines his destiny." It's important that talk be unrestricted. Team members often feel safer when conversation falls within familiar territory, but deep, open and uncomfortable talk is better for growth and strengthening bonds between members. Don't miss out on this powerful way to get closer. It can be very nourishing. Initiate new topics. Dream out loud. Explore different subjects. All things are helped immensely by talking openly.

Learning how to talk deeply creates a rare and wonderful *energy*. Close and healthy teams are built through frequent, honest two-way conversation with one another and lots of it. Cultivate the ability to talk about everything. Teach every team member the value of totally open communication. Don't restrict the boundaries of conversation. Let team members know it's okay to grow individually in different areas and directions. Be open, direct and deep. As leaders, we must help foster and continue the dialogue. Describe problems, give information, encourage discussion and don't forget to model how it should be done. Fully express your own thoughts, feelings, needs and expectations. This includes sharing flaws. Talk about everything. Share past experiences and what was learned from them; it will inspire team members to share theirs.

Encourage your team members to engage in this open talking on a regular basis. Establish a ritual where all team members go around the table and talk about the most meaningful—or discouraging—professional part of their workday or week. This may be about an event with a client, a team project frustration or a creative idea—anything that has special importance. Happy as well as difficult experiences can be shared during this time. If done consistently it will have a powerful impact on your team's interpersonal relationships.

Old and New Leadership Paradigms

The old management paradigm was to roll with the punches—don't express yourself emotionally because it meant you were weak. Distance yourself—be arrogant! But now, leaders need to be engaging, self-effacing, unpretentious, endearing and charismatic. Yes, these are all attributes that can be learned, developed and practiced by leaders.

The new leadership paradigm asks you to portray your total self. Express yourself emotionally, show enthusiasm, excitement and concern about others to express that you *really* care. Add texture to your relationships so that employees and managers link and bond. Show personal warmth, pulling others in by being a good listener and asking questions. This type of emotional depth and communication builds and lifts up individuals and teams.

Establish an Emotional Connection

The numbers on a balance sheet will change and a stock price will fluctuate, but an emotional connection will resonate long after the statistics fade. Contrary to popular belief, it is not financial reward that inspires greatness. Great leaders find a way to connect with others and inspire the unique strengths within each team member. It sets up a pattern that says you turn to others to help solve problems—it's not on your shoulders alone. The team can share the problem.

Establishing an emotional connection is a great way to create meaningful points of contact among team members. These connections set up interpersonal "channels" that link members of a team together and super-charge common growth and collaboration. People feel good about turning to others and getting engaged.

Make your presentations exciting and invigorating, and fire-up your teams with enthusiasm. Check out how you present yourself in your everyday life at work and the image that you give off. Engage in two-way dialogue, create open energy, shift the paradigm and establish an emotional connection.

CHAPTER 15
USE HUMOR

"At the height of laughter, the universe is flung into a kaleidoscope of new possibilities."

Jean Houston, American author involved in the "human potential movement"

The Theory and Benefits of Laughter

There is a sect of Zen Buddhists that begin their mornings with fifteen minutes of laughter every day. They say that the remainder of their day falls naturally into its proper place from that point on. A good laugh not only gives quick energy but also lets the body relax and release stress. Take all the angst and intensity that come with life's ups and downs and balance it with the power of laughter and the joy of play. And remember that fun—whether in the form of flexible work schedules or playful pranks at work—improves a person's temperament and productivity.

You may want to keep a book and record your team's funny adventures. Recalling these when times are serious can bring in some frivolity and the lightness of a fresh perspective when you need it most. Call it your team's journal of adventures. There are funny stories in all organizations.

The medical benefits of laughter are often noted. Giggles relieve stress, control pain, lower blood pressure, provide an aerobic workout for the diaphragm, improve the body's ability to utilize oxygen and maximize the flow of disease-fighting proteins and cells to the blood. Laughter strengthens the insides, physically and emotionally. Telling tasteful jokes and doing funny things should be encouraged by everyone. The insides need these emotional releases, and those daily doses of giggles are best learned from those coworkers who are funny! Keep them near.

In our task-focused world it is easy to overlook that there is a reason why studies show children learn best through play. Don't forget that adults learn through play too. Isn't it odd that work is supposed to be very serious? To our point: all team members must learn to nurture more laughter and play on the work front. Let's take a look at several organizations that do this well.

Two Examples of "Corporate Laughter"

Southwest Airlines

If you haven't been on an airplane with funny Southwest Airlines flight attendants, we hope you will very soon. These folks brilliantly infuse comedy into their daily work lives. They certainly add a little bit more "joy" to the process of reaching your destination.

Southwest Airlines was founded on these admirable values: Work should be fun—enjoy it. Work is important—don't spoil it with seriousness. Humor is at the core of Southwest's culture. The company's "people department" or personnel department even uses humor as one of the hiring criteria for its employees.

Red Frog Events

Red Frog Events is an event production company and pioneer of the experiential entertainment industry. Employees have exceptionally innovative titles that reflect their fun-loving culture. They believe that a more relaxed, authentic form of communication is most effective, and extend this sentiment in turn to their customers. A good sense of humor pervades the organization.

Their descriptive titles are not only creative, fun and inspiring, they also lead to informal ways to interact and do business. Employees are called "froggers." Here are a few "frogger" titles: Promoter of Passion,

Juggler of Justice, Constructor of Chaos, Tackler of Talent, Headmaster of Heart, Duchess of Details and Cardinal of Collaboration.

The two co-founders, Astronaut Joe Reynolds and Master of Monkey Business Ryan Kunkel, also have imaginative titles. They shared with us their early-on thinking behind the choice of a unique "business cards" and their resourceful people titles. "Our business cards are metal bottle openers! This sets the tone to be at ease doing business with us." We agree—a bottle opener would, most certainly, promote dialogue! They continued, "Our titles are less about individuality and more about shared values. Whether it's our race director meeting with a permitting office in Texas, or our concert planner reaching out to individual bands to arrange the musical agenda for our Firefly Festival, frogger titles set a tone about who we are and why we are different." A bottle opener "business card" and an imaginative business title are terrific examples of ways to nurture and promote a more relaxed culture and at the same time foster humor.

Red Frog encourages something that "froggers" refer to as "cry laughs." This is a condition that they describe as "laughing so hard your eyes tear. Symptoms are heightened during late work hours, tight deadlines and outdoor event extreme weather. Treatment is sleep." Their entire team or "frog family" nurtures a culture where laughter is part of their success.

A good sense of humor is an essential tool for surviving the ups and downs of work. Develop, use and share it! Use imaginative tools and humor to promote relaxed communication such as innovative business cards and emotive business titles. Use laughter to counter stress and nurture productivity, especially during late work nights and tight deadlines.

CHAPTER 16
CREATE A PERSONAL
LEADERSHIP PLAN

*"Always remember that you are absolutely unique.
Just like everyone else."*

**Margaret Mead, American cultural anthropologist and
our professor at Columbia University**

What Is My Unique Leadership Style?

Let's be clear—the new leader is *you*. Our entire goal for this book is to enable you to put a self-development plan in place to become a more effective leader and lift people up in your organization. We want you to find and unlock the gleaming, multi-faceted leader inside you. In this section we share a five-tiered approach to help you unleash your leadership spirit, unlock the secrets of success and open up new channels of discovery. This is a step-by-step blueprint to help you lead your own teams or organization. It will galvanize your values, norms and desired leadership style, and should help to detail your action plan to create a vibrant, inclusive and collaborative team and culture.

1. Personal leadership vision.

The starting point for a personal leadership plan is the vision that describes your desired leadership style. Where do you want to go? What will you be doing? What will it feel like? What is your dream? A vision statement allows you to make decisions based on whether or not they are consistent with what kind of leader you see yourself becoming. A *personal leadership vision statement* answers two questions:

- How do I want to lead?
- What will it feel like?

Vision statements should define a specific point in time – one or two years down the road. Importantly, effective vision statements are congruent with your goals, needs, strengths, values and norms. An example vision statement is: "In two years from now, I want to express more compassion, collaborate more with others and convey greater mutual respect to better align my team to our values."

You may want to describe your vision specifically by leveraging our six leadership qualities of humility, compassion, transparency, inclusiveness, collaboration and values-based decisiveness. For example, "In two years from now, I want to convey a collaborative and transparent leadership style and make decisions by incorporating the views and opinions of others."

2. Awareness.

This is intended for you to think about who you are as a professional. Consider your needs and wants, and how you can achieve your professional passion—the things you like to do the most. List at least two to three answers for each question below:

- Who am I?
- What are my needs?
- What are my professional passions?

3. Self-discovery.

A vital step towards personal growth involves gaining a better understanding of the self. What is my greatest strength that can be brought to the team? What weaknesses need to be shored up? When do I disappoint members of a group? How can I really motivate a team member?

Talents are your mental and physical strengths. We were either born with them or developed them over time. Reflect on your own individual strengths and weaknesses.

We recommend that you ask several peers, mentors and leaders for their comments on your strengths and weaknesses as well.

4. Individual values.

Values are those principles and ideals that we hold passionately and deeply. They express what is most important to you—what you value or place above everything! Make a list of your own values—your beliefs that you want embodied in your work environment. Some of our own personal values are: consideration for others, respect for all individuals, humor, deep listening, open-mindedness, compassion, family togetherness, creativity and innovation.

5. Building group, team and culture norms.

As detailed in earlier chapters, norms are the actions that activate desired values. Once you have a clear vision of what kind of leader you want to become and which values are most important to you, it is time to determine the necessary actions or behaviors to make that vision a reality. Describe what efforts need to be undertaken to build group norms, a sense of teamwork and a shared culture. Fine-tune how you will reach out to your teammates.

- **Group Norms**—What leadership behaviors should be activated? What specific communication style will I use?

- **Team Dynamics**—As a leader, how do I build an effective team, connect with colleagues and create a sense of community?

- **Reach Out to Others**—How do I inspire others to bring out their core strengths and talents?

- **Culture**—How do I build a set of shared values? How do I facilitate cultural fit, retention and loyalty at work?

6. How do I get there?

Now that you have your vision statement, awareness, self-discovery, individual values and group norms, you need to figure out how you are going to bridge the gap from where you are now to where you want to be.

1. Figure out which specific strategies will help you get to your vision. Come up with three or four strategies. Each should be concise. For example: I will go to a communication course to improve my compassionate listening skills.

2. For each strategy, what are the important tactics – the who, what, when and how? Focus on the essential details to make each strategy happen. For example, take a week-long course in New York on how to give effective speeches and gain media presence and exposure from a former TV producer.

3. Identify obstacles and needed support. Ask yourself: What obstacles am I aware of and how will I overcome them? What support do I foresee I will need, and how will I ask for it?

You can use our six steps above to design your own Personal Leadership Plan (PLP). Importantly, take time to fine-tune your PLP. You may find yourself spending a week or two revaluating and making changes. When you are finished, write it up and be prepared to share it with your team leader and mentor.

Customize A Personal Leadership Statement

The best leadership plan is a highly personal one. Adam Hecktman, Director of Technology and Civic Innovation for Microsoft, created a personal leadership statement and set of values to communicate his commitment to his team members as their leader. Adam describes his need for what he called his personal mission and management statement: "I was doing some career soul-searching. It was nothing more than a few sentences, but it took me time to finalize." It was designed to enable and empower both employees and teams. His mission states: "I promise to my team that I will help you out. My job is to tell your story." He had learned from his team members that they felt they were not getting the recognition they deserved from their customers, so part of *his* mission became to recognize them for their hard work. Addressing his team's feelings of under-appreciation, "my mission is to earn the trust of my team every day. Be present, watch them work, know what they want to get out of their job and help them grow their career. I can only tell their story if I know things on that level." Adam described a deep connection: "I love my team. It is genuine love. I want to do what's best for them— and doing what is best for them is doing what's right."

Ultimately, personalizing and sharing a mission statement like this can build trust and re-engage a team leader and his or her peers. "There was a time when they were losing faith in me. I rebuilt our trust."

The Personal Leadership Plan will help unleash the leader within you by defining self-awareness needs, values and norms, strengths and weaknesses, and leadership goals and strategies to get there.

SECTION

3

CREATE A
HIGH-PERFORMING
CULTURE

CHAPTER 17
BUILD CULTURE FROM
THE GROUND UP

"Culture isn't the most important thing. It's the only thing."

Jim Sinegal, Costco President and CEO, 1983-2012

Organizational culture can be extremely hard to change. Not only is it difficult to define something so intangible, but it can be challenging to identify the appropriate steps to turn a desired culture into a reality. Culture can mean different things to different people. For some, it has to do with how employees communicate with each other. For others, culture is about the look of an office or how their company views work/life balance. For Brian Bannon, CEO of the Chicago Public Library, "Culture is the combination of the attitudes and mindsets of the people and partners that help us contribute to fulfilling our mission. People who work here, even though we are a large legacy institution, are here because of a strong sense of mission. Lives have been changed through our work."

Culture—both in nonprofit and for-profit organizations—has a direct affect on an individual's productivity and motivation. However, for some reason many companies don't take the time to assess and analyze their culture to see how it can be improved or better tailored to their organizational vision and goals. Most teams or organizations have never written down how they go about their work, interact with others, organize, reach important decisions or select and care for their employees. Yet we all have this detailed knowledge within us. Each of these examples and more are components to an organization-wide culture, and we share a general understanding of it without thinking or talking about it directly.

What Is Culture?

Culture is the shared knowledge that tells us what is important (values) and how to act (norms) in a particular environment or setting. A group's culture tells its members what they need to know so that others within the group will accept them and support their actions. This specific "cultural information" is developed and learned within the group. It enables members to read the behavior and events that they observe, and better relate to others. When employees don't carry the same cultural information, watch out! One can see the conflict coming from around the corner. Culture must be developed and shared from the ground up.

It takes time to learn and understand the cultural details of any group or organization. A culture is powerful and pervasive, but extremely subtle as well. Organizations, much like individual countries, form unique cultures. In fact, the culture of each organization is different and unique. Amanda Lannert, CEO of Jellyvision, talks about having a quirky culture. Every new employee gets a standing ovation at the end of their first day on the job. Lannert says, "we know it is awkward, and we know you're scared, but we want you to know we're glad you're here."

A cover article in the September 2017 *Harvard Business Review*, entitled "Work and the Loneliness Epidemic," says that despite our increasing connectedness, society is seeing rising levels of loneliness. This epidemic is not only harming people's health, it's also making employees less productive and engaged at work. To improve the workplace, former US Surgeon General Vivek Murthy argues companies need to focus on building social connections. "Our understanding of biology, psychology and the workplace calls for companies to make fostering social connections a strategic priority," he writes. To our point, a shared culture creates a sense of belonging and serves to reduce isolation at work.

While culture can be created based on intent and design, too often it develops unconsciously without a concerted effort or focused vision for what its members want the culture to become. Forming a culture involves developing and sharing a common set of beliefs (values), norms (behavior guidelines), attitudes (points of view), goals (plans for the future) and information (detailed cultural knowledge). That's why culture needs to be consciously cultivated by every member of the organization—all the way from the CEO down to the lowest level employees. It must be a collective effort of all the people who work there.

Resistance to Change

The benefits of creating a shared and collaborative culture are significant. Once achieved it creates a sense of belonging, and employees feel that what they do is important. It generates more cohesion among team members and aligns everyone along the commonly agreed upon values and norms that have been set.

So why exactly is culture so difficult to change? We have discovered five reasons over the years that enable its hard-to-alter feature.

1. It is a human endeavor. People are inherently resistant to change
   in all aspects of life, and corporate culture is no exception.

2. It is in our heads *and* our hearts. It requires a balanced connection between our logical reasoning and our emotional feelings, which can be challenging.

3. It arises from shared knowledge and behaviors. Getting everyone in the organization aligned on accepted values and norms can be
   a very difficult task.

4. It is self-reinforcing. The longer a system or culture is in place, the more difficult it will be to uproot the status quo and make significant change.

5. It is a powerful, invisible force. It can be difficult to draw attention to the intangible and convince people of the value brought by an improved culture.

Mirror and Transform Culture

Mirroring is the process of becoming part of a culture by living the group's values and practicing the group's norms again and again until the behaviors are finally automatic and habitual. It enables the culture of the group to solidify and grow over time. In order for this to occur, team members watch carefully and listen intently to the spoken and unspoken signals that individual members use to interact with each other. Once they have observed the rituals of the group, they begin to mirror or imitate the behaviors they have observed until they become second nature. In this way, they learn and adapt to their particular team or organizational culture's uniqueness, peculiarities and eccentricities. Mirroring can be a great tool for new employees to quickly become better acquainted with a culture.

Unfortunately, most traditional leaders want their employees to mirror the existing corporate culture rather than participate in transforming and evolving it. Culture needs to embrace the values of all employees—not just the values of a few people at the top. Wrongfully, we often see that senior executives want employees to merely observe and imitate rather than filter, enrich and interact with new cultural information they receive. Under this scenario, the sparkling insights and perspectives of other employees and members don't have a chance to develop and be added to the team culture. Instead, members become engrained in the habit of mindlessly adopting the current cultural norms. These are the types of places where you'll often hear questions from an employee like "Why is it done that way?" or "Why didn't you include me in that decision?" or "Why aren't people willing to try that unique idea?" The typical response is, "Because that's just the way we do it around here."

Many of us have experienced authoritative corporate cultures where employees have learned that no one should ever say anything "negative" at any time. Meetings become show-off times, where employees or team members only report positive news—how much revenue has been brought in or how many points scored in sales commissions. But the downside of this type of culture is that there are no opportunities to express doubts, brainstorm, try out new ideas or express more than a very narrow range of emotions.

Sharing a mistake and what was learned from it would not fit into this corporate culture. Such expressive behavior is considered inappropriate, not to mention the vulnerability associated with sharing a failure. The employees had to learn this cultural norm through experience and trial-and-error. An individual's natural way of expressing creative ideas, doubts and thoughts may have regenerated the culture or helped it evolve in a positive way, however they were encouraged to mirror this negative norm and not alter the status quo. The norm created a negative feedback loop that only worsened the situation.

Why shouldn't employees have a say in the norms and values of their culture? If we close ourselves off to their input because they're just "new" or "young," we disempower them with the belief that their values aren't important to the rest of the organization. The culture of a company should include the desired norms and values of <u>all</u> its members. If you think this is way above the heads of younger or newer employees, ask some of them what their values are. You'll be pleasantly surprised by their insights.

Setting Culture Up from the Start— The Red Frog Perspective

Chicago-based Red Frog Events is an award-winning event production company. Their incredible growth is due, in part, to the care and maintenance of a rare and strong culture. Having a defined culture helps their company hire employees, measure success and guide business strategy. We learned in our interview with its two co-founders, Ryan Kunkel and Joe Reynolds, that from the beginning they focused on crafting an innovative culture.

They carefully created and set in place a visionary document called "The Red Frog Way" which states: "We boldly agree to make a positive impact on the world, be the crown jewel of our industry, and stay healthy and thriving for 100+ years. Bringing this vision to life takes passionate people and a shared way that unites us. We call it our 'Red Frog Way,' and it's the secret sauce that leads us onward and upward."

They support this cultural vision with six shared values:

- **Heart**—It begins with kindness at our core.
- **Grit**—With resilience and contagious optimism, we push forward.
- **Entrepreneurial spirit**—Ask 'why.' Dream big. Dive in. Make mistakes. Repeat.
- **Red Frog Proud**—Those soak-it-in moments when it all comes together.
- **Frog Family**—Road trips, growing pains, occasional cry laughs and not letting each other fail.
- **Individuality**—We celebrate it.

Importantly, as the company grows and employees develop, the culture needs to be routinely reexamined and tweaked. Stressed the two co-founders, "It is a misconception that you can achieve a good culture and move on. Culture-building ebbs and flows, evolves, reacts and adjusts continually. The vibe we have today shouldn't be the vibe we have five years from now. You are going to have different personalities and skill sets, and the workplace has to display this evolution." We strongly agree. While it is crucial to set up and devote considerable time to a start-up culture, leadership must be mindful and ready to update the values, norms and "tenets" periodically as the culture evolves. Otherwise, the organization risks "outgrowing" its culture and creating a discrepancy between how the culture used to operate and how they should today.

The secret to Red Frog's innovative culture has been to cultivate leaders at all levels and empower each one to fan the company flame. Co-founders Reynolds and Kunkel shared: "We both have very high standards. We expect a lot but we give a lot in return. We genuinely care about each person and fight hard to make the right business decisions to support them as individuals, empowering them to make decisions and identify with our company's strategy and goals. When they have a bad day, we always try to make it right." There you have it! These two remarkable co-founders are examples of peopleship leaders in action. They treat others as individuals; recognize their strengths, likes and dislikes; listen to others' ideas and nurture a sense of trust and inclusivity.

Heat Up the Culture Pot

Every Christmas Eve our family makes clam chowder. It has become a permanent part of our holiday traditions. An observer of our kitchen scene might be surprised at our industrious and methodical activity. The five of us participate equally in preparing and cooking our chowder. We have a huge pot for this, the very sight of which primes our taste buds for our scrumptious and savory stew. Together, we cut and blanch the bacon, chop and sauté the celery and onions, and dice the potatoes. Everything is added to the pot. Tomatoes are optional, and strong feelings surface every year as to whether or not we put them in. Other essential ingredients include chicken soup stock, canned minced clams and hot milk, which we thicken with a roux mixture of flour and butter. We also add ground black pepper, thyme leaves and garnish with parsley.

The thing is, we all know what's in our chowder. Any one of us could make it without the cherished recipe. Yet to be sure, with five "chefs" assiduously involved, our chowder never tastes quite the same from year to year. Once, the roux wasn't added to the hot milk at the right time and it curdled. Another year, we tossed out the clam juice instead of adding it to the pot! And another time we undercooked the potatoes, discovering that they weren't tender nor mushy enough for our taste. Despite each year's slight "attention" to the recipe, we've learned that if we are sure to add all the different ingredients, the flavors will still blend together and taste sensational.

Your team or organization's culture also needs a good-sized pot. There must be room for each member's unique and personal ideas and contributions. Employees want to feel valued and have the opportunity to proactively contribute. Examples include: "Let's all play a role in marketing the firm." "Let's launch an effort to become more community service-oriented." "Let's take one day during the week to do something totally creative and different after work." If employees are involved in "cooking up" their organization's culture, then heartier, healthier and more vibrant relationships are sure to simmer for everyone to enjoy.

Like our annual clam chowder, know that your work culture will be an ever changing, always transforming creation—especially if you have lots of chefs! Decide on the ingredients together. Mix them up. Experiment. Don't forget to pour in large measures of essential ingredients like equality, ownership, accountability, encouragement, shared-leadership, humility, inclusiveness, service, respect and creativity. Toss in a lot of humor too. These will always make for hearty relationships. Warm them up, and enjoy! A rich work culture can serve its members for a lifetime.

Culture is the shared knowledge that members carry around in their heads and hearts. Form yours thoughtfully. Every member should have a say in establishing and changing the values and norms of the organization.

CHAPTER 18
INSTILL VALUES

"There is no hierarchy of values by which one culture has the right to insist on all its own values and deny those of another."

Margaret Mead, renown cultural anthropologist and our professor at Columbia University

We discovered that companies often have acronyms to outline and share their values. At Cleversafe, they use TRICK, which stands for Trustworthy, Results-oriented, Innovative, Customer-focused, and Knowledge-driven. At SoCore Energy, they use HHS, which means Humble, Hungry and Smart. At Alberto Culver, they use RESPECT, which stands for Rational, Entrepreneurial, Strategic, Passionate, Encouraging, Collaborative and Trustworthy. Each of these sets of values paints a unique framework for the culture of its respective organization. They are all poignant, powerful and succinct. But how did these companies decide which values were right for them? Where did they come from?

Identifying Shared Values

Values describe a person's beliefs, ideals and goals. They embody an individual's judgment on what is important in life. They evoke strong inner convictions. They are what a person cherishes most. Values influence the choices and decisions we make, the way we invest our energy and time, the people we choose to be close to and the interests we pursue. In difficult times, they serve as a compass to guide conversation and decision-making amid conflicting demands and varying points of view. Before we can lay a foundation for a culture that is real, meaningful, satisfying and applicable to an *entire* organization, we must know more about each person's unique set of values. In other words, the starting point to creating a company-wide culture is a basic awareness of individual values and the forces that shape them.

Team members have their own unique values, and it is crucial to let them surface organically. It can be helpful to have each member of your team write down his or her values and share them with each other. Write yours down too, but be sure not to impose *your* values onto your team! Each person must discover, identify and own their values—try to eliminate bias and prevent team members from simply replicating what the rest of the room is saying. Although this identification process sounds simple, it requires some serious thinking and reflection. Once team members have identified their intrinsic values, leaders should be sure to recognize the strengths and merit of their members' values, acknowledge and support the values cited by their team members and encourage open discussions on the topic of values.

Take a very close look at each team member's listed values. Each person should try to select at least five top values and write them down. Then, have each team member talk about his or her values with everyone listening deeply. If a team member has clearly identified her values, she will be able to better handle important decision-making opportunities and have greater comfort when taking risks, all because she knows what is deeply important to her. She will see what interests and priorities outweigh others and will be stronger because of it.

Understanding your fellow members' values is what creates greater harmony within a group. There is awareness and clarity on what's important to each member, and from this leaders can better understand where members' strengths lie. Use this information to help plan how to allocate expertise and resources in order to get the best possible use out of a team member's time.

Mutually agreed-upon values link employees together without the need for bureaucratic rules, corporate regulations or hierarchical organization structures. In fact, these oppressive, top-down approaches to culture creation have the opposite desired effect. Instead of aligning employees to a corporate strategy, they create barriers to creativity and enthusiasm. To be meaningful, these values must be generated from within—from the bottom up. Shared values and norms are the glue that connects employees to each other and to the organization. When they are in place, employees get exhilarated. They become fired-up.

The Values Identification Process

We have some tips or "tricks of the trade" to keep in mind when writing up your organization's values. We have paired each of these tips with an exemplary value from Zappos, the online shoe company acquired by Amazon. All Zappos employees have these values deeply engrained in their psyches and have committed them to memory. Their commitment to incorporating these values into their daily lives is what helps Zappos create a truly enviable corporate culture.

Tips for Describing Your Values	Zappos' Values
(1) Align your mission and values	*Deliver WOW through service.*
(2) Use descriptive language	*Create fun and a little weirdness.*
(3) Begin with an action verb	*Embrace and drive change.*
(4) Stay away from meaningless, boring platitudes, don't overuse company jargon and avoid long-winded, in-actionable values	*Build a positive team and family spirit.*
(5) tay away from values that have a lack of resonance with stakeholders	*Be passionate and determined.*
(6) Keep values simple	*Be humble.*
(7) Have values be part of the daily life—not just a plaque on the wall.	*Be adventurous, creative & open-minded.*
(8) Keep the list short (rule of thumb, 3-10)	

This values identification and adoption process is a lot easier said than done, so let's explore the process of building an organizational set of values based on its constituents.

Step 1: Individual values development

We begin with the recognition and development of personal values. Leaders should send a letter describing the purpose of their initiative, and hold a series of small-group workshops explaining the process to the entire team. Everyone involved needs to gain an understanding of the purpose, intended impact and benefits of this values-aligning endeavor.

The group leaders should ask team members to write down their personal values that they would want to embrace and be shared by their co-team members in the organization. If you really want to get your hands dirty, have them also list what they perceive to be the values of the current team or organization. This can give a lot of great insight into what changes need to be made.

Step 2: Prioritize the top five to ten values

The next step is to ask individuals to prioritize their own top values, indicating which ones they would like to see in their workplace. They should select three to five personal values they'd like to see activated on a daily basis and then share with their co-workers.

Leaders should next gather up the top priority values of all team members and publish a list of the collective responses. Usually, most individual values end up falling into a distinct number of broad categories. Even small organizations might find that there are broad groupings of values. For larger organizations, it may be helpful to do a more detailed analysis on the responses to determine the frequency of most commonly cited values. Individual values can then be segmented according to divisions, functions, teams and other organizational divisions if applicable. For example, in a highly decentralized organization, comparing the similarities and differences among subsidiaries may be beneficial and help establish mini-teams. Similarly, the separate schools of a large university might have differing values that can be segmented and better aligned. No matter how the values are grouped, the important part is making sure you get insights from everyone in the organization from the very bottom to the top.

Step 3: Review individual values, rank top priorities and develop a core set of values

Once individual values have been identified and prioritized, then we can progress into the small group work phase. Leaders should form small groups consisting of eight to twelve individuals and one or two managers. We find that some of the best groups are those that cut across several vertical layers of managers and employees. It is important that there be multiple meetings on the topic of group values within each small group; this can't be done well in just one sitting. Facilitators should be prepared to:

- *Review individual values and rank each group's top value categories*. In the first meeting, group facilitators should help members review the previously published individual values and identify the most important categories.

- *Develop a core set of values*. Next, and most important job of the group facilitator, is to concentrate on developing a list of the specific values that each group wants to adopt. These will eventually become the organizational or group's value pledge.

Step 4: Generate Organizational Values Pledge

It is now time to assemble the prioritized values that the entire organization will embrace. The impact of these values will be humongous. To some degree, these values need to support and codify the basis for promotions, rewards, leadership style and interaction with others. This is one of the ways that we show employees and team members that these values have weight.

It is important to remember that there are no right or wrong statements regarding organizational values. Making the values statement credible is absolutely essential. Unless employees believe and see management act and behave in ways that reinforce the agreed-upon values with their own eyes, they won't put forth the time and effort necessary to activate those values.

In some companies, we've seen top management write up an Organizational Values Pledge, announce it to all employees and then watch it fall flat on its face. That's because the only way to build authenticity into a values pledge is to have all employees and management build the pledge together. It's not rocket science; the Organizational Values Pledge must capture the core values desired by the entire organization. Without broad participation, active listening and thorough integration, the pledge may actually do more harm than good. Once employees see management give lip service to values, all future credibility is lost.

Making the time investment to develop values can bring meaning to employees and their jobs. Management must express a strong commitment and support for the values adoption process. There needs to be a fundamental respect for and trust in all individuals, beginning with a basic interest in including all employees in the process. Employees invest their lives in the workplace; they need to feel that it's worth it. They need an invitation to participate. Developing a core set of values gives them this invitation to help actively shape the future of their organization.

Encourage team members to identify and prioritize their values—then share them as a group by creating an Organizational Values Pledge.

CHAPTER 19
IDENTIFY NORMS
TO WORK BY

"Most conduct is guided by norms rather than by laws. Norms are voluntary and are effective because they are enforced by peer pressure."

**Paul Collier, professor of economics and public policy
at the University of Oxford**

There are two main dimensions to an organizational culture. As we have discussed, values serve as the foundation for what leaders and employees want the culture to embody. Values describe what is important to people, and give the guidelines for how people should treat each other and expect to be treated themselves. The other side of the culture coin is norms. Norms are the actions that people take on a day-to-day basis. They cover everything from communication practices to what time people show up to work in the morning.

What is the relationship between values and norms? In effect, norms serve as the "translators" of values into daily behaviors and communications. Norms are group-decided codes of conduct. Without them, values can end up just being a list of beliefs. As we all know, actions speak louder than words. The values are the words; the norms are the actions. Values are internal—within individuals; norms are external—demonstrated by individuals.

As the cultural development process gets under way, team members may need to be clear on the context for developing a Norms Action Plan. Norms are expectations about behavior that are shared by the members of a group. They are social rules, written and unwritten, that specify what behavior is appropriate and what is not within a specific culture. Norms serve as a means for guiding individual actions so that they coincide with the actions of others. They act as a social blueprint to create mutually agreed upon actions among group members.

Through time and practice, norms become social standards or goals to which we align our actions or behavior. They dictate conduct in formal and informal situations. They tell us how to behave and what to say in and out of staff meetings. Norms emerge when a group, through its own experiences, identifies a particular behavior to be good or bad for its members. If the behavior is good for the group, it is encouraged. If it is bad, the group discourages or even forbids it. A norm can apply to how employees act throughout an entire organization or it can be specific to a particular team or small group. They define the shared expectations of the group. A Norms Action Plan, then, is a process that fosters the creation of behavioral guidelines specifically designed to match the values adopted during the Values Adoption Process. The two go hand-in-hand when developing a values-based organizational culture.

Examples of Norms

In any organization we need to identify the desired set of norms and behaviors that we want all employees to live by and act on daily. Once identified, an organization then needs to develop a concrete and tangible "tool box" of rewards that will reinforce or discourage different behaviors. The key to this endeavor is to identify the norms that exist today that the culture wants to reinforce, as well as new norms that don't currently exist but will be essential to support the desired values. For example, "convey genuine care about others" may be a norm you'll want to keep, while "provide frequent feedback on a 360 degree basis" would be a new norm that you'd want to add.

Similarly, you'll need to identify norms that you'd want to discourage or eliminate—like taking credit for someone else's idea, discouraging the expression of someone's opinion or forcing others to conform to a certain style.

It's important to remember that like values, norms are uniquely tied to a particular organization. Sonny Garg described the behavioral norms within the engineering culture at Exelon. "Our norms are driven towards scale, processes efficiencies, reliability and zero tolerance for failure, operational excellence and financial discipline. Do it really well and for as cheap as possible. Our industry is safe, reliable and affordable, that's what our customers want." Powerful and definitive, Exelon's norms are clear cut and not something to mess with!

Norms Identification Process

The actual process of creating a Norms Action Plan (NAP) is nearly a mirror image of the Values Adoption Process. Similar to the Values Adoption Process, NAP facilitators should hold an iterative series of small-group discussions with employees to create the desired norms as well as ideas for appropriate rewards. In addition, senior management will need to approve and endorse the NAP because many of the actions will likely impact compensation and overall personnel policies.

The five steps for developing a Norms Action Plan are described below. As with the VAP, several of these steps occur nearly simultaneously in the initial stages of the NAP. The careful facilitation of each step becomes increasingly important as the NAP process unfolds. A successfully implemented Norms Action Plan has the power to provide an enormous energy "kick" to an organization.

Step 1: List desired current norms

Ask each employee to list the norms and behaviors that their organization currently endorses and that they, as individuals, want to be further reinforced. The list should comprise the top five to six behavioral norms that are most important and meaningful to each employee. The norms should support the individual's values, serve as a source of satisfaction and provide a sense of belonging to the group.

Here are some examples of some desired norms cited by employees who have done this in the past:

- Starting and stopping meetings on time; being punctual conveys respect of others' time and commitments.

- Providing positive feedback and constructive criticism throughout
a project instead of evaluating performance after the project ends.

- Giving both verbal and written comments on performance to provide encouragement.

- Offering frequent training to employees to customize their developmental needs.

- Keeping time commitments made to other team members.

- Establishing team bonus programs that reward the value of team contributions and performance.

Step 2: Describe current norms to discourage

Next, have employees list the current organizational norms and behaviors that they dislike and would prefer to eliminate from their workplace. They should come up with a list of the top four to five behaviors that should be discouraged or frowned upon. These norms are typically categorized as those that create a demotivating work environment.

A few examples of norms to discourage that surfaced in our research include:

- Patronizing employees or "putting them down."

- Putting in "face time" at the office, not productive time.

- Speaking disparagingly about co-workers.

- Masking feelings and emotions about an issue for fear of reprimand.

- Promoting employees based on how well they "manage up" rather than how well they produce quality work.

- Communicating only through written memos rather than directly in person.

Step 3: Define new norms to create

Employees should identify three to four new norms that they would like to have others adopt as daily practices to guide their behavior, interaction and communication with co-workers. These should be norms that most people in the organization currently do not convey or activate. An example of a new norm that frequently surfaced from our research was using more descriptive praise to nurture desired behaviors and achievements. This can be an especially useful new norm because the more it is used, the more other positive norms are called out and encouraged, creating a great positive feedback loop.

A few other examples of new norms that surfaced in our research include:

- Confronting people tactfully.
- Reaching out to customers to meet their needs.
- Giving more frequent praise.
- Supporting cross-functional teams.
- Allowing employees to have flexible hours.
- Designing a reward system that is linked to performance.

Step 4: Determine unacceptable norms

The final set of norms that should be talked about is the three to four behaviors that are wholly unacceptable. When we use the word "unacceptable," we mean those practices that, under any circumstance, would be enough to cause an employee to leave the organization voluntarily. There very well may be more than three to four norms that are viewed as extremely unattractive or that must be eliminated for an employee to feel good about his or her work environment. However, the task here is to identify the top three to four behaviors that are indeed totally unacceptable.

Here are some examples of some unacceptable norms cited by employees who have done this in the past:

- Discriminating

- Harassing

- Lying

- Yelling

- Lacking consideration and respect for others

- Discouraging others from expressing their opinions

- Forcing others to conform to one leader's authority

Step 5: Generate norms pledge

Facilitators should lead a lively discussion to identify the norms that are desired by the group, as well as those undesirable norms that they want to discourage. Facilitators should capture all suggestions. Then, the group should summarize and rank those high-priority norms to professionally live and work by. Norms should be finalized, distributed to each member and shared within the team or organization in the form of an "Organizational Norms Pledge."

To recap, the Norms Action Plan (NAP) builds on the Values Adoption Process (VAP). Crafting the NAP defines norms that will reinforce the desired values and works to translate them into behavioral actions and attitudinal mindsets. Values alone won't cut it. Behavioral and communication norms must be established to provide tangible and concrete signs that bolster and activate desired values.

Norms are collective behaviors that reinforce desired values. Encourage team members to identify and prioritize their norms—then share them as a group by creating an Organizational Norms Pledge.

CHAPTER 20
THROW FAILURE PARTIES
AND CELEBRATE SUCCESS

"Our greatest glory is not in never falling, but in rising every time we fall."

Confucius, Chinese politician, teacher and philosopher, born 551 B.C.

Nothing enables progress quite like failure. Accepting and working through failure is an enormously important part of effective cultures. When we fail, we are given an opportunity to learn from our mistakes. We can analyze what went wrong and why, and use that knowledge to improve everything we do onwards. We're talking about "smart failures" here. If completed with ample preparation and a comprehensive strategy, a project that totally fails can at times end up providing more long-term benefit than a mild success.

What does this mean for leaders? They must build a culture where the freedom to take risks, experiment and fail is accepted. They must nurture a willingness to analyze and learn from failure rather than "punish" the one who took a risk and failed. They must stretch us, take us further than we thought we could go and encourage us to try again if we fail. Real progress and prosperity are the results of learning, and one of the best sources of knowledge and insight is failure.

To be clear, we're not advocating that organizations try to fail in attempts to gain learning and insight. Instead, our goal is to encourage leaders to embrace calculated risks and diminish the fear of failure. Organizations need to create a portfolio of different innovations with varying degrees of risk. Yes, of course, it is coming up with creative, innovative ideas and solutions. But it is also recognizing that the idea-generating process is inherently difficult, and failure is an intrinsic part of discovery and innovation. Even successful new product and service companies experience a forty percent failure rate of commercialized new offerings. CEOs who accept, understand and broadcast this, enable a "risk-takers will be the victors" attitude. Mistakes will be made, however the willingness to accept smart failures will instill confidence in team members and over time generate higher financial results. Now that is a victory you can't beat!

Because failure is so crucial to achieving goals and reaching success, why not celebrate failures with a party? Most leaders give lip service to accepting failures, and a valuable way to show commitment to risk-taking and convey an acceptance of failure is to hold failure parties! That's right; host an elaborate, fun-filled affair with all team members who worked on the project. Take the time to debrief the project in a light-hearted manner, and discuss what went wrong and what could have been done in retrospect to improve the end result. The key is to give people permission to fail and learn from those failures so the mistakes won't be repeated.

Another way to plan for and mitigate risk is to build failure into your financial forecasts. If you are looking for $12 million in new innovation revenues, then you need to launch $20 million worth—applying a 60% success rate to reach the goal. One of the most common mistakes we see is when companies plan for an unobtainable 100% success rate.

Making discovery and innovation happen requires large amounts of courage. Leaders must create environments where risk-taking and innovation are part of the team and organization's mindsets. Leaders must be willing to stick their necks out, stay courageous and continue to pursue the project. There are long-term benefits in charting a course to explore innovation. By celebrating failures, you convey to your organization the understanding and acceptance that risk-taking will yield a mix of successes and failures.

Praising Failure

Praising someone for failing might seem counterintuitive, but as prominent cultural anthropologist, Mary Catherine Bateson, describes: "It seems to me that in a situation of potential peril, one of the things that paralyzes people is the fear of doing the wrong thing. So when they act, some kind of reinforcing response is well worth doing, even if what they did was not successful."

In thinking about praise and its role in "firing" up success, Bateson stresses, "It is important to realize that when a person's behavior is positive, it is easy to praise. When it's negative, you want to suggest an alternative. But there is also the middle position, where team members play it safe and don't do anything. You don't want to evoke or encourage that behavior. It is useless." Her take away: the fact that someone was present, tried and contributed needs to be acknowledged, whether or not they were successful.

Leaders have to value and support the courage to fail. If a team member has been working on a project for a year and comes back with a recommendation to *not* develop it, the leader has to be able to say, "you know, it really helps that you have given this a full exploration. You persisted and looked at it, and you had the courage to say 'I don't think we should follow this road,' and that's great!" Now that response breeds success.

Using Disciplined Freedom

"Freedom is nothing but a chance to be better," said the French writer, Albert Camus. We agree. Leaders need to give teams the latitude to make mistakes and learn from them. Leaders must trust the team. There should be a delicate balance maintained between rigor and flexibility, analysis and creativity, teamwork and individual achievement, and discipline and freedom. You cannot have one without the other.

When there are uncertain paths ahead, it's important to maintain something that we've coined "disciplined freedom." It means that employees have distinct guidelines and expectations, but also have the freedom and creativity to choose multiple paths to get to an end result. Disciplined freedom provides team members with a sense of autonomy and entrepreneurialism, while giving them adequate direction and operating guidelines to help guide their decision-making process. It suggests that team members can think for themselves and use intuition, previous experience and business judgment to make important decisions. It supports an environment that respects the views, opinions and ideas of each team member. Disciplined freedom fosters a vibrant and energized team that is motivated to innovate and think differently.

Delegating responsibility and full accountability to team members creates more individual commitment and buy-in. As long as a sense of freedom is felt, participants are more likely to stand up for and develop an attachment to a concept. Colleagues, in turn, feel more comfortable conveying emotion, enthusiasm and passion.

Too often, enthusiasm is judged as a frivolous emotion. Not true. Passion is a critical ingredient for sparking innovation. This passion or emotional freedom is harnessed by having a clear strategy, process, set of screening criteria and financial goals in place. The road map should be defined, but there must be some flexibility for the drivers to take a variety of routes to reach their destinations. The more choices they make, the more entrenched they become in the project. By the end, team leaders and members are fully invested in their innovations, and speak about them with noticeable passion and gusto.

Many leaders focus on creating a sense of urgency. They think that the right way to achieve a result is to establish deadlines. Similar to a "stretch" goal, the well-intended leader thinks that forcing a team to meet an unrealistic launch date will serve as a catalyst to motivate them. All this technique does is demoralize the team and weaken the process, usually resulting in failures. Doing the right amount of up-front homework, spending more time on testing and conducting sound analysis for a new concept will yield better results than eliminating steps to save time and hasten the launch date. There has to be a balance between doing the right things and doing things right. In the long run, spending adequate time on each stage in the development process saves time rather than wastes it.

Disciplined freedom provides parameters that enable team members to feel comfortable working without fear of risking their careers. This freedom trickles down to team members as leaders are more comfortable encouraging members to be mavericks, be contrarian and express emotion. Together, the team can piece together bits of information, inputs and data to assemble the puzzle, which eventually reveals a plan.

Express Vulnerability and Clean the Slate

"The best leaders have shown me that it is okay to say 'I don't know,'" shared Carol Bernick, former Chairman of Alberto-Culver. "The best thing you can do is never be afraid of questions. And when you don't know the answer, make sure you get back to people when you figure it out. The best leaders I have seen show emotion. They connect with their people. They are not afraid to show them that they are vulnerable."

To "clean the slate" means to let go of our past mishaps, hardships and negative experiences. Hanging on to past grievances, unfair practices and hurtful relationships do no good. Admit your mistakes and the mistakes of others. Forgive yourself and others who have intentionally, or more often than not unintentionally, harmed you. Start fresh. Work through some of the past "baggage" or "unfinished business." An open and accepting mindset will better enable you to embrace your new leadership construct and definition of success.

It's Okay to Make Mistakes— Don't Search for Perfection

"I live with a fear of failure," said one head of a Fortune 500 company. "Failure to me is when I screw up or let somebody down. I once had an associate who was under performing; she didn't have a clue what she was doing and we had a sales meeting coming up. I ripped into her in front of six or seven of her peers. The team felt terrible she felt terrible and I knew I had disappointed all those people who thought highly of me. My personal failures occur when I step outside my values. I value respect more than anything. Yes, she was wrong and doing a lousy job but that was no reason to humiliate her. I disappointed myself and I disappointed everyone on the team. That occurred more than ten years ago and I still think about that mistake."

For this CEO, his greatest failures are not defined by financial returns, they are much more personal. They are what he views as betrayals of who he is and the values he wants to represent. It is these moments, the rare instances when he steps outside of his values that haunt him. It is these moments that remind him why his values are the foundation of all his decisions.

"Somebody once shared with me the philosophy that 'ninety percent is an A,' and I think that is a helpful perspective," another leader said. "I am always trying to be a perfectionist and that gets me into trouble sometimes. If you look at your friends and pick them apart, you can always find something that you don't like. You just have to remember that ninety percent is an A. Now if a person falls in the sixty percent range, I don't have much time for them. In my personal relationships, in dealing with our highest executives, I don't have to agree with every-thing they do or say as long as we can come to a ninety percent agreement." Mistakes happen. This is vitally important to recognize not only for yourself, but also for those around you. This leader understands the most important thing is not to search for perfection, but rather to search for a shared foundation.

This excellent practice facilitates collaboration. Understanding that no one is perfect and that ninety percent is good enough creates a greater willingness to collaborate. When the leader or team member makes a mistake, forgive and forget it. Everybody is wrong some of the time.

Free to Fail

The prize is different now. Organizational leaders need to create a learning culture that leverages individual strengths for the benefit of the whole. That means the freedom to take risks, experiment and fail. More importantly, it means the willingness to analyze and learn from failure rather than "punish" the one who fails. This means developing a working environment where leaders are supportive. Leaders must stretch us, take us further than we thought we could go and accept us back to try again when we fail.

> *Failures are the kindling and fire for future victories. Praise failure. Know that disciplined freedom is an essential part of a team leader's mindset. Clean the slate and don't expect perfection.*

CHAPTER 21
ENVISION YOUR
FUTURE CULTURE

"Without involvement, there is no commitment.
Mark it down, asterisk it, circle it, underline it."

Stephen Covey, author of
The 7 Habits of Highly Effective People

One way to build buy-in and commitment to an innovative culture is to create a "Declaration of Culture." Simply put, this is a tangible document that states the vision, desired shared values, norms to activate and the intended impact of the culture relative to growth goals and mindset. It can be short and concise. Importantly, all senior management *must* sign it. An enhanced level of commitment and buy-in comes from physically signing the document. Often times executives are reluctant to sign it as it signals to the entire organization that they have agreed to commit to the declaration, and this only reinforces the power that signing the document can have in transforming a culture.

Examples of Shared Values

We want to share some examples of organizational values that cut across different types of businesses and sectors. They include shared values envisioned by the culture at the Dupage Children's Museum, Google, IBM, Qualfon, 7-Eleven/Mexico and Alfa. While these organizations represent wildly different industries, each was able to develop a tailored values-driven culture. It really goes to show that any organization has the power to develop a positive culture for its constituents.

Dupage Children's Museum

Each member of the Dupage Children's Museum team in Naperville, Illinois has one value in common: a dedication to providing learning and fun to all who visit. Founded in 1987 by two early childhood educators, Louise Beem and Dorothy Carpenter, the Museum started out as a van that traveled to park districts, scout troops and preschools. Several years later, when it opened in a temporary location, museum workers had to take exhibits out of a storage area each morning and assemble them, only to reverse the process at the end of the day. Twenty years later, DCM was named one of Chicagoland's top 10 cultural attractions by *Crain's Chicago Business*. Today the DCM has three floors of interactive exhibits, innovative programs and events, and fun Learning Labs to meet the needs of the children and communities it serves.

The Dupage Children's Museum's desired culture and vision is still the same—to create a world where there is the time and space for all children to reach their full, unique learning potential through hands-on play. DCM's shared values focus on respect for all children and their ability to learn, the power of play as a basis for constructing knowledge and the importance of the child-adult learning partnership. Specifically, their core values include:

1. Respect for everyone
2. Collaborative teamwork
3. Open and honest communication
4. Creative, flexible and stimulating environment
5. Fun, playful and positive energy
6. Encouragement of risk-taking

Google

Google has a unique innovation-friendly culture. Often listed as a *Fortune* magazine "Best Company to Work For," the company has standout cultural qualities. Google's focus is on its people—it treats employees as owners. It empowers employees by believing everyone can have an impact. Transparency is king and queen; a weekly TGIF gives employees the opportunity to ask questions to the CEO directly. Perks galore prevail, including free gourmet food, an annual ski trip, dog-friendly offices, massages, nap pods, laundry machines, errand cars, 18-week maternity leave and full benefits for partners. Last but not least, engineers can spend twenty percent of their own time pursuing projects that spark their interest—that's one whole day per week!

Here are Google's shared values:

1. Innovation comes from anywhere

2. Focus on the user

3. Aim to be ten times better

4. Bet on technical insights

5. Ship and iterate

6. Give employees twenty percent time

7. Default to open processes

8. Fail well

9. Have a mission that matters

IBM

One might think that a company with 320,000 employees across the globe would have logistical difficulties with a values identification process. The former CEO, Sam Palmisano, launched a creative solution to combat this—a free-flowing, seventy-two hour online dialogue called a "values jam" which took place over a weekend. Its purpose was to examine the "stuff" getting in the way of serving clients. Three shared core values emerged for IBMers to adhere to going forward:

1. Dedication to every client's success

2. Innovation that matters, for our company and for the world

3. Trust and personal responsibility in all relationships

Sam Palmisano states, "If there's no way to optimize IBM through organizational structure or by management dictate, you have to empower people while ensuring that they're making the right calls. I'm talking about decisions that support and give life to IBM's strategy and brand, decisions that shape a culture. That's why values, for us, aren't soft. They're the basis of what we do."

Qualfon

Qualfon is dedicated to being the best Business Process Outsourcer. Business process outsourcing involves the contracting of the operations and responsibilities of a specific business process to a third-party service provider. Qualfon is unique in the BPO industry in that its mission is to "make people's lives better." And it does! Susan Kuczmarski was the keynote speaker for Qualfon's annual leadership summit in 2016. She discovered a powerful and unique culture, clearly defined not just by its shared mission, but by a unique set of pervasive values and norms. These are further developed and nurtured by Qualfon leaders who are encouraged to be messengers, mentors and managers.

Six values permeate Qualfon's culture:

1. Encouragement
2. Dignity
3. Integrity
4. Service
5. Results
6. Teamwork

To enact these values, Qualfon employees embrace ten norms:

1. We embrace cultural diversity
2. We are willing to endure
3. We are a trusted and loyal partner for our clients
4. We stand shoulder to shoulder
5. We are determined to always improve

6. We are a second family

7. We focus on people first

8. We live joyfully

9. We are faith alive

10. We think big

7-Eleven/Mexico

Another company that stands out in Mexico is 7-Eleven. Its culture is defined by a unique set of shared values, which include:

1. **People**—Value each person's dignity, maximize his or her potential and generate the best place to work.

2. **Customer service**—Do anything to satisfy the changing needs of our customers and consumers.

3. **Passion for results**—Guarantee results with speed, flexibility and opportunity.

4. **Innovation**—Find new and better ways to do things.

5. **Integrity**—Always act according to our principles.

6. **Teamwork**—Ensure participation, collaboration and commitment of everyone and among each other.

7-Eleven/Mexico also developed norms for each employee to follow. These behaviors were creatively displayed for all to see. Worn around the neck, a stiff small card pinpointed "dos and don'ts," and provided guidelines for each store employee. Specific behaviors were color-coded: green behaviors were encouraged, red behaviors were not allowed. It was hard to miss the pervasiveness of these norms. This creatively displayed "reminder" was one of the finest that we have seen.

Alfa

Alfa is one of the largest companies in Mexico. Their work has a massive footprint throughout the world. Not only are they an important producer, marketer and distributor of food through recognized brands in Mexico, the United States, Europe and Latin America, they are also one of the world's largest producers of polyester. They are a leading producer of innovative light-weight solutions for the automotive industry, as well as information technology and communication services for business, government and residential markets. Despite the varieties of business units and sectors served, Alfa still manages to maintain a shared culture that filters through the organization from the corporate level all the way down to each of the different businesses.

Alfa's shared values are something to shout about.

1. **Integrity**—Our actions are governed by our commitment to ethical conduct and social responsibility.

2. **Respect and Empathy**—We consider diversity as a strength. We seek to incorporate individuals with different backgrounds and experiences. We aspire to provide a work environment that promotes trust and cooperation.

3. **Results Oriented**—We are committed to value creation and to the continuous improvement of our businesses. All our employees embody a personal commitment to improving the performance of the company.

4. **Innovation and Entrepreneurial Approach**—We encourage and reward innovation and development of new business opportunities.

5. **Client Based**—We are dedicated to exceeding our clients' needs.

Alfa's values are a powerful model for other organizations. They live and breathe their shared values. They provide a reason to believe.

To create buy-in and commitment, create a "Declaration of Culture" that is signed by senior management. To help envision a desired culture, check out and be inspired by what other organizations have put in place.

CHAPTER 22
THE BENEFITS OF CULTURE

"It is not necessary to change. Survival is not mandatory."

W. Edwards Deming, American engineer, statistician and scientific pioneer of quality control

The intangible nature of culture is what makes it so hard to define and manipulate. It can be very challenging to change something that you cannot see with your eyes or project on a graph. Because of this, there can be a disconnect for many in terms of how something like culture can be a major benefit to an organization. The balance sheet has space for assets and liabilities, but no line item for culture. The immense benefits an organization can yield from a positive, innovative culture are often overlooked because senior leaders and shareholders don't get quarterly reports on culture-related initiatives and their impact on success.

However, culture affects every single person in an organization and is one of the most influencing factors on how efficiently employees will perform. Sandee Kastrul, founder of i.c.stars, also believes that culture drives performance. "I define culture as the people, experiences and conditions that create our view of the world. The people are our team— the staff, stakeholders, interns and managers. These people touch and are touched by i.c.stars. The people side of culture is fluid and always changing."

Benefits of Culture

How would you describe the benefits of a culture? David Ahrens, chief marketing officer at Tradeshift, shares his insightful answer. "When you are in an innovative environment, in a weird way, everyone relaxes!

There is so much excitement and people with high energy levels, people perform better, their shoulders aren't down, people give more, people believe in themselves more. You get a much more confident organization—and in the corporate world, confidence is everything. Culture changes the game."

Adam Hecktman from Microsoft offered his perspective on the benefits of their culture: "You are never bored to work here. I can never keep my attention on one thing very long. It is constantly motivating. It is what has kept me in this company for a quarter of a century. It speaks both to the culture and the fact that we innovate on top of it. I don't know that there has ever been a period of time where we have innovated this much, and this publically, which is keeping me excited."

A more positive and free-flowing culture creates an environment where employees are engaged, motivated and perform at their optimal levels.

What Role Does Culture Play in Growth, Sales, Profit and Motivation?

Ultimately, a culture of innovation can lead to faster growth, higher profits and more success. This can come from new ideas, greater efficiency and more motivated employees. To this point, John Berschied, formerly with Alberto Culver, describes how innovative cultures offer more benefits to an organization. "When the culture is innovative, you are tapping into the total knowledge of the entire organization as opposed to selected bits and pieces. I have seen so many times that the squeaky wheel gets the grease. That's all well and good, but you have these other people over there that might not be as vocal about it, they still need to be encouraged because you need their knowledge as well. If you don't tap into these folks, you are disempowering these people and allowing them to get less involved, less motivated and less likely to contribute in the future."

Performance and motivation are a two-way street. If you, as a leader, are going to expect the most out of your employees, it is imperative that you develop a culture that encourages and enables them.

Close Relationships Shape the Culture

At Cleversafe, the developers have close relationships. They have their own vocabulary and know one another very well, which has created a tightly-knit and collaborative atmosphere. Shares the founder, Chris Gladwin, "Employees are the culture. We have never lost a key developer. These guys are friends. It helps to build true friendships and relationships. Innovation is not just some guy sitting in a closet with a light bulb going off over his head. It's a team of knowledge. We have our own vocabulary."

Collaboration is a key enabler of innovation, and when an organization can make it a cornerstone of their culture, it is sure to breed new ideas, strategies and platforms. It allows the employees to develop a culture that is a culmination of their individual values and norms, and naturally creates a synergistic environment for teams. As these relationships become closer and more intimate over time, teammates will gain a better understanding of each other's nuanced strengths and weaknesses. They will know who to ask for help and guidance, and when to step up and take leadership over a particular aspect of a project. This is how a collaborative culture can turn a group of individuals into a well-oiled machine of a team.

"Measuring" Culture

How do you measure a successful culture? How do you qualify an intangible? Some choose not to. David Ahrens shares his method for measuring culture: "I quantify it in the most non-quantifiable way. When you walk into a company, the culture is different if there are sparkles in people's eyes. In an innovative culture people are excited, and you have a strong belief in a shared vision. There is a 'we can do this' attitude that is pervasive. It is not orchestrated, but a lot of *natural energy* exists. To me, these are the markers that define a successful innovative culture." Ahrens doesn't feel the need to quantify cultural success because he knows it when he sees it, and he understands the value it brings. He postulates, "could you measure more quantifiable things? Could you tie the success of an innovative culture to revenues or new product launches? Of course, but these human metrics of culture are the most important ones."

Unfortunately, not all senior managers are as easily convinced of the value of these "intangible" metrics. Luckily, there are ways of tying culture metrics to tangible things like financial returns too. If your culture is devoted to creating innovative new products portfolios, then the revenues from those market launches can be used to justify a successful culture shift. Or, if your latest cultural initiative involves improving customer service, you can measure its success through increases in customer loyalty or growth in market share. At Hyatt, Jeff Semenchuk describes how he measures their innovation culture through a combination of tangible and intangible metrics. "You see it behaviorally. People engage with each other, there is laughter, they are smiling, they are relaxed and energized, there is openness and there is a free flow of everybody participating. You also measure success through things like speed of doing things. Things seem to get done quickly. If there is a lot of critique and criticism, this is a bad sign. Proactively questioning and building up are good signs."

Have the Right Team

Building the right team is essential to success. It can often be difficult to decide who to hire and if those people are a good fit. Linda Mallers, founder of FarmLogix, expressed this concern: "With the *wrong* team you can't grow. The culture isn't aligned. When you decide to change the team, it makes everyone feel secure. Then, you have to walk people through why you did what you did. We have to share everything." As to her biggest fear, "It's finding the right people as we continue to grow and building up our middle management structure to support what we are doing. I have to make sure that the infrastructure is in place that will support these customers and new people. It is my responsibility to continue to execute. Can I keep scaling it and doing it at the level I'm doing today, which will be critical for our success?" Getting the right team in place and giving them a voice is crucial for growth and success. They steer and fuel the engine.

Have the Right Structure

In our interviews with other executives, we learned something insightful: keeping innovation at the top and having senior executives make all the decisions on which new products or services to launch will stifle the entire innovation process. Hierarchical organizational structures are problematic, as they create inequalities. Pete Kadens, founder of SoCore Energy, tried to make these hierarchal structures less apparent by eliminating dress code, executive offices and what he described as the "bullshit and politics" that come with hierarchal structure.

When new innovations are decided upon only by senior managers, it sends a message throughout the organization that no one else can participate in it. In turn, others are demotivated. They never see any benefits to finding innovative ways to do things. David Ahrens has worked with many large companies. Through his experiences, he has seen this ivory-tower mentality all too often. "Innovation was often relegated to the senior executives, who sat with flip charts and white boards in the executive-only boardroom and even with the smartest people, failed repeatedly. They didn't make innovation part of the entire culture. It was the most amazing thing you've ever seen. Even with the best ideas and the brightest folks in the room, it's not going to work unless everyone is behind it." Bottom line: to spread a culture of innovation throughout an organization, all individuals, not just senior management, must be involved.

Flatten It Down

In order to mitigate the barriers of the over-hierarchical structure, we recommend a two-fold model: fewer layers and little-to-no hierarchy. These "old" arrangements organize power to the leaders at the top. Authority is squirreled away by those few who were in positions of power. The new model calls for hierarchy demolition. Interdependent networks replace hierarchy and set the stage for effective teaming. These mutually supporting networks distribute power to team members in the workplace who add value. Now the growth and self-worth of individuals who "live" in teams is supported.

When the workplace is flat, team members care more about others, both within their team and among their organization as a whole. They learn to listen, and listen to learn. Individual team members don't simply focus on "who am I?" and "what are my needs?" but they are also aware of "who are you?" and "what are your needs?" Rather than mindlessly follow a leader, team members lead themselves for the benefit of the group and, ultimately, the organization. This type of shared leadership builds self-esteem and confidence, which better enables team members to express their explicit points of view and become stronger participants. With this focus, all team members become leaders. It's the new way—peopleship.

Flat organizations tend to be more participative and supportive, and often cultivate a sense of ownership and trust in others. Team members can spend more time on personal relationships. Together, leaders and group members build a strong culture through common values and norms, shared leadership, agreed-upon goals and a common identity. Building and maintaining a strong sense of togetherness requires leaders and employees alike to be concerned with the future.

In order to open new doors and grow for the future, we need to think beyond what already exists. Most people are scared of the unknown. For peopleship leaders, however, the unknown represents opportunity; it represents the future. While others shy away, these leaders run toward the door, anxious to be the first one through.

Focusing on Your Values and Your Personal Greatness

During difficult times, leaning on your personal values can be invigorating. Relying more and more on the things that you naturally do well also provides solstice, guidance and direction.

Our values allow us to distill things and focus on what is really important. In this way, we are able to maximize our strengths. Turning to our values provides us with the channel to satisfy seemingly competing demands. Personal values are not picked from a book or pulled from thin air; they reflect our personalities and behaviors. As such, reliance on our values allows us to perform more effectively.

Working on what you are passionate about is also crucially important. We think you make the most difference with your time on this planet doing more of what you care about versus what you are good at.

Dealing With People

Try to reach down into the organization. Deal directly with people. Meet people on their turf. Let people know all your little imperfections. It can have a genuine impact on morale. Employees are excited to work with people that they have easy access to, who share their expectations and fears and listen to them.

The more you treat people as individuals, the more successful you will be. Values are uncompromising, but the way in which you convey them to other people can—and should—vary.

We are big believers in that your leadership changes with each person that you deal with; you can't manage ten people all the same way. Hold on to your principles, but certain people need more room, and others less.

Valuing Progress Over Results

Results: everyone in business wants them. They measure, benchmark and set deadlines. However, with this focus on the end result, the journey along the way is often forgotten.

Too often people say, "I want to get from A to Z and if I'm not at M by this date, then I have failed." The main thing is, "am I moving forward or learning something really important for the next round?"

Leaders understand that if an organization is learning and a team is growing, then there is no true failure regardless of the results. The most important goal is *progress*, because over time moving forward is the only thing that will consistently deliver results.

> *There are enormous benefits to an innovation culture— from revenue and profit growth to employee respect and close relationships. Morale and happiness are measures of a successful culture. When you build the right team and a more flattened structure, you will find innovative, energized and more productive people who value progress.*

INDEX

Index